# AUSTRALIAN SUMMER

# AUSTRALIAN SUMMER

## *ENGLAND'S TOUR OF AUSTRALIA*
### 1936–37

NEVILLE CARDUS

SOUVENIR PRESS

Printed in Great Britain by
Billing & Sons Ltd., Worcester

TO

SIR KEITH MURDOCH

# CONTENTS

# CHAPTER I

# THE BACKGROUND

I AM afraid I have waited too long before finishing this book, which, according to first intentions, should have described in set terms the tour of the English cricket team through Australia in the season of 1936–37. As I write, I am on board the R.M.S. *Orontes* sailing back home; the cricketers are returning by New Zealand and America; at last I am alone and unobserved. But for the life of me I cannot fix my mind on the Test matches, and I am glad I gave attention to them day by day; I could not possibly see them in detail now, or feel their sweep and action. As the ship goes unhurriedly through the Indian Ocean, and as the ocean seems hourly to increase and become the whole world, my imagination beholds Australia shrinking away behind, until it achieves that pathos of distance, and even of smallness in isolation, which for me are the sources of affection. The other night we put forth from Fremantle; we had for nearly a week been hugging the shores of Australia; it is nearly three thousand miles from Sydney to Fremantle. But now we really were, at last, taking farewell of the country. And as I leant over the ship's side, and watched the coastline receding, and as I saw the lights twinkling on land, my heart suddenly ached. I saw in a quick vision the whole of the Australia I had traversed since October. I saw the red night-signs of Sydney; the falling of Brisbane's mantle of twilight; the cosy intimacy of Adelaide; Melbourne's *bourgeois* geniality. I saw six months of my life concentrated, so to say, in a map of

9

Australia now rolling up, perhaps for good and all, for me. The end of a chapter and of an ambition!

When I was a small boy, running wild in the streets of Manchester, I read a book on cricket, in the Free Library; it was by P. F. Warner. One of the photographs depicted Adelaide Oval in the sunset. 'I shall go there some day', the urchin told himself; he might as well have said, 'I shall be Prime Minister some day'. Last November, as I hope to tell later on in these pages, I went to Adelaide Oval on a morning of rich sunshine. And there I sat next to Clem Hill, a hero of my boyhood. I used to pay sixpence to watch Victor Trumper and Clem Hill at Old Trafford. I once stole a volume of Coleridge's poems out of my grandfather's library and sold it to a second-hand bookseller for a shilling; this shilling enabled me to see Trumper make a hundred before lunch in the three-run match of 1902. (I remember that when I went to sell the volume, feeling a criminal, I noticed one of the poems was called 'Remorse'; to this day I cannot understand how the poems got into my grand-father's library, which began with the Bible and ended with the *Sporting Chronicle Handicap Book*.) That year I waited outside Old Trafford to look at Clem Hill and worship him; in those days, small boys never dreamed of approaching their gods for autographs. Wonder and glory of life, I sat at Adelaide Oval, next to Clem Hill, last November as ever was!

When an ambition of a lifetime is fulfilled, when a boy's dream comes true, something has gone from one's life; I can never again cross the seas to Australia for the first time, never again tread for the first time an Australian cricket field and say: 'Here it is—here's the place I've dreamed on, and seen in sunshine, far away under the earth, under my bed, on cold winter nights, in England';

never again see for the first time the beauty of the Heads at
Sydney, or walk to the 'Gap' and see for the first time the
ferry lights across to Manly, and hear for the first time the
lap of the water around the old *Captain Cook*, the tug which
rests in the curve of Watson's Bay, where at night beauty
comes out of the sky and the water holds it.

I hope my book will give some idea of the changing
picture of these last six months. I was unhappy in Australia
at the beginning, or at any rate uncomfortable—out of
joint, with the need of all my humour (and William Pollock's) to keep my spirits going. The place seemed so far
away from the world, not only as a fact of geography and
distance; there was apparently nothing here of the things of
the mind, no music, no theatre, little reflective talk. I of
course committed the usual embracing generalizations of
the Englishman abroad (and Australia *is* abroad, an unusual
civilization, English only by accident of blood relationship).
I said to myself: 'This is a crude land, young and raw and
maybe likeable, but entirely out of the zone of the world's
history, culture, and tradition.' There is truth in this, but
my mistake was not merely one of emphasis; it sprang
from lack of knowledge and a wrong point of view. After
all, what impressions would an Australian obtain of Eng-
and if he visited it in an English summer, with a cricket
team? Where, between May and September, outside of
London, would he find a good concert, a good play, after a
day of sport? Australia's position in Time and Space makes
it hard for people there to sustain efforts towards a way of
living and thinking not external; the climate directs the
mind's eye outward; people are constantly going somewhere or doing something, playing a game or wallowing in
the sunshine or the surf on the beaches. This is a happy
land. The first thing that strikes the English visitor to

Australia is the carefree, almost reckless, high spirits of everybody. Even a failure by Bradman causes only a momentary depression. People get concerned about you if you spend any time alone; they think you are sickening for something, and they proceed in a body to do something hearty about it. The life in Australian homes is genial, and they are very beautiful homes too; in England we live in pens or hovels. Australian family life is much what family life was in England in the days of our grandfathers; you must live with the Australians, in their homes, to understand why in a city of Sydney's or Melbourne's importance there are few restaurants, and those only for people going to cinemas; the meal is consumed hurriedly to satisfy hunger. Australians have little sense of the ritual of dining out.

The general setting of the land makes for out-of-door activity; you can go weeks and not share conversations based on abstract ideas; it is all about practical things—events, projects, achievements. In this way Australia is indeed young, vigorous of limb and outlook, rather too prone to the dogmatism and the narrowness of the young. During a Test match season, cricket is the common passion —but we'll come to that in this book, in God's good time.

My book, whichever way it takes or turns, will, I hope, show that the cricket was not the whole of the adventure; that Australia, like any other country, needs to be known, and has a genius for friendship; and that it has no need slavishly to imitate English, American, or European notions, but has its own character, derived from its environment. Australians often seemed ready to apologize that Australia is 'still in the making'—which reminds me. I found in most Australian hotels a certain noisiness at midnight; a man with a hammer would begin to strike some hard metal substance outside my bedroom window; this happened in many different places, at Adelaide, Melbourne, Perth, always shortly after midnight. So that once in an argument, when an Australian protested at something I had more or less innocently remarked, and said: 'But remember, Australia is only in the making', I replied: 'I am never likely to forget it: I hear them making it every night under my bedroom window'. But in these days the country is lucky that seems worth hammering together at all, and has some stuff there to be hammered.

By this time the cricketer is no doubt wondering whether my book ever will turn its attention to the game; I ask him to be patient; I promise that some order and point will emerge gradually from my discursiveness. I wish to present the Test matches in their setting, for to me cricket must be put against a background. Lord's is Lord's because of what it stands for in matters that are beyond the scoreboard's power to show; nobody will get the flavour of a Lancashire and Yorkshire match if he does not understand why Bramall Lane is different in character from Trent Bridge. I shall try to relate the Test matches to the Australian scene as I saw it and lived in it. I shall make the effort, even if I am compelled after all to relegate the cricket to an appendix.

# CHAPTER II

## LEITMOTIV

WHEN the team walked up the gangway to the *Orion* at Southampton on September 13th, a sudden torrent of rain drove everybody headlong into the ship. This was the Leitmotiv of the tour, for wherever the team travelled they broke droughts at sight. In every match, almost, rain seriously influenced the play, and at Melbourne rain decided the main issue. Rain fell at Sydney as soon as the cricketers took the Sydney train from Melbourne; this was the first rain in Sydney for six months. Even at Brisbane, clouds came one evening into a sky which for days had contained only naked merciless heat; in tropical straight lines the rain descended, opening the dry earth, making life come again to trees and flowers. Next morning England won the first Test match on a soft pitch, though the fact should be stressed at once that England had got a firm hold on the match before the change of the weather. At Sydney, another downpour allowed Allen to declare his innings closed, and break the back of Australia's first innings on a pitch soft on top and hard underneath. At the time—as we shall see from the narrative of events—the Australian batsmen were severely taken to task for their incompetence on moist turf; there was an outcry against the custom of covering the wicket. I myself joined the condemnation and shared the opinion that our own batsmen would have done better than the Australians in circumstances which are normal to an English summer. There was a nice irony waiting us; England lost the rubber by helpless batting on

14

Melbourne's stickiest wicket, and not only that, but in the fifth Test match, where the pitch was rather akin to the 'flying' wickets at Sydney and Brisbane, the English bats-men no more liked rising fast stuff than the Australians had liked Voce and Allen during the two games in which fortune apparently placed the laurels for good and all most fulsomely at Allen's feet.

Sardonic imps fooled us prettily. Hammond began well and petered away; Bradman began as though riddled with fallibility, then at the right moment displayed a precision even more inhuman than that which we saw in England in 1930. The English batsmen were certain at Brisbane that they had mastered O'Reilly; on the scorching Sunday morning after the Saturday of the Test match there, I walked across the street from the Queensland Club to the hotel where the players were staying. I saw Allen ready to depart for a day's bathing and he said: 'Whether we win this match or not, we'll win the rubber. We've got O'Reilly down; he can't spin his leg-break.' At the finish, O'Reilly was once more the greatest medium-paced bowler of the present time. Allen played splendid all-round cricket until Christmas; with the advent of the New Year, his luck shamefully deserted him. He had to work too hard, on the field and off. At one period, even Charles Fry lagged behind Allen in speeches made in public, and the only difference between private and public speaking, as far as Fry is concerned, is that in the second instance an audience is formally present. England's collective strength declined as Australia's increased; at one period Allen was carrying six or seven half-failures—Hardstaff, Worthington, Fagg, Fish-lock, Robins, Sims, and Ames as a batsman (but Ames as a wicket-keeper was admirable throughout). To win a rubber in Australia an England team needs a technical superiority of say thirty per cent. The accidents to Wyatt and to Robins had serious consequences; Wyatt would have guaranteed solidity in the middle and perhaps at the beginning of the innings, and perhaps Robins would have provided some serious leg-spin. Still, despite everything England should have won the rubber, even after the defeat at Melbourne in the New Year, and even after the return to form of Bradman. A negative batting policy at Adelaide played into Australia's hands.. These points will receive underlining in the diary of happenings. On the whole, Allen and his men emerged from the Test matches as skilfully as any of us expected them to do when last September the cloudburst at Southampton hinted of the wrath to come.

# CHAPTER III

## ON THE WAY

LIFE on the ship during the voyage out was not according to my expectations; I began it with some romantic ideas lingering in my mind since my boyhood about the talks and intimacy which would occur amongst a company of cricketers setting forth to play Australia. The team merged with the rest of the passengers until you scarcely knew where they were or which was which; Allen rightly encouraged his men temporarily to avoid cricket. The fun of the voyage was at times not easily to be marked off from the fun of a fashionable hotel on any evening at Folkestone after a day at the September festival. It became boring, and I gladly escaped from it. I even left the captain's table—not disrespectfully, I hope. The captain was charming and a marvel of tact. But the time arrived when I was ready either to laugh outright or become sarcastic at the efforts of the social climbers who each evening vied with one another to obtain the captain's recognition. The snobbishness on an ocean-going liner is appalling. 'I imagine that most captains in the service would like at times to leave the captain's table. But this is another digression.

When we reached the Red Sea, I decided to begin a diary; I did not keep it up, of course, for the simple reason that on a ship nothing often happens; Mark Twain achieved the perfect summary:

'Oct. 13, Got up, washed, went to bed.
„ 14, „ „ „ „ „ „
„ 15, „ „ „ „ „ „

17

and so on and so forth.' My own entries are a little fuller; here they are:

*September* 25        ON THE *Orion*

'Passengers may sleep on deck in the vicinity of the forward lounge between midnight and 6.30 a.m.'—so runs, with much confidence, the notice that has to-day been given prominence in the various premises of the *Orion*. We are in the Red Sea as I write, and there is scarcely a soul on board, not including the ship's cat, who is capable of any form of sleep, either on deck or below the deck, in cabin or under the starry heavens; the Red Sea is at its hottest, its stickiest, its cruellest. There is no air in the world, except fetid breath from the desert; the *Orion* makes not a wisp of a breeze as she goes her patient course. The sun is merciless, and when we escape the chastisement of its fiery rods by going under awnings or inside the lounge or drawing-room or tavern or café, then we are suffocated, or, rather, put under some evil drug of the Orient. There is one place only where we can find momentary release from the torment—in the dining-room (only we don't want to dine), where the atmosphere is marvellously chilled. Here the temperature is 75 degrees, and as we enter it we feel as though we have gone into a refrigerator; we expect, even hope, to see frost and snow appearing over our bodies. When at last we reluctantly leave the dining-room and pass out through its swing doors, we go straight, without a second's break, into an oven.

I have never before dreamed that the world could become so hot, that people could endure such miseries, that nature could go its ways so indifferent to mortal needs. For three days the sun has hurled down on us the light and heat that destroys; for three days the sky has contained not a cloud, nothing but the pitiless blue of endless and indifferent space. And hour by hour the sea has grown hotter, so that at night, after the sun has gone down and a lovely silver horn of a moon has enchanted the sky, even then we have had no peace, for the waters hold the day's scorchings and throw them back. 'Passengers may sleep on deck'—may, indeed! I did not try; I kept to my cabin and hopefully manipulated the device that blows air upon you, risking sore throat, stiff neck, double pneumonia. Anything would be better and more merciful than to 'pass out' from Red Sea humidity, either by oozing away or by going mad and diving overboard with such despair that one hit the floor of the ocean and perished as much from concussion of the brain as from drowning.

The other evening, a quarter of an hour before dinner, I met Captain Howard on the staircase; the manager of the M.C.C. team had only ten minutes ago changed into his dinner jacket. His collar was already a rag; Mr. Gladstone, after four hours or so of eloquence, never more drastically reduced stiff linen to this state of shapeless wetness. From the foreheads of all of us waterfalls have descended, splashing and dashing like the cascades of Southey's poem. (Was it Southey?—it is still too hot to think here, though at last we are emerging from the Red Sea and a breeze is stirring, giving us a sense of resurrection of all the world from the dead.) At the first hint of this heaven-sent zephyr R. W. V. Robins stripped off his evening jacket and, regardless of dignity and braces, went to the promenade deck and, feeling the faintest suggestion of a wind, said to me: 'We seem to be cooling as we direct our course towards the Antarctic'. Robins has suffered much and has borne it all with humour and an Alfred Lester sort of fortitude.

Everything that science can do towards the defeat of the

Red Sea is done on the *Orion,* but nature, as Mr. Squeers said, is a 'rum 'un'. 'She's a lovely ship,' said Hammond, 'but I wish she—well had wings!' I tell of these hardships not out of a desire to present ourselves as martyrs and heroes but to console those we have left at home on the brink of an English winter. 'Lucky you!' they said as we departed from Southampton a fortnight ago; 'oh lucky, to be going into the sunshine, while we shiver in the east winds and hug our hot-water bottles!' At the moment of writing, there is scarcely an English man or woman on the boat who would not cheerfully give pounds and pounds sterling for one hour of Manchester's wettest rain and coldest cold. Happy days are probably waiting for us in Australia—we shall deserve them, for we have suffered in the Red Sea's cauldron. But such is human nature that while we were writhing and dissolving in the Red Sea, we persuaded ourselves that the Red Sea was really behaving with unusual moderation; then the moment we sniffed a wind of the Indian Ocean we agreed unanimously that the Red Sea had broken records in heat and life-destroying humidity, and we went about amongst ourselves distributing medals for patience, endurance, and philosophy, so to say. The probability is that we revealed ourselves as so many comfortable creatures of the temperate zone of the earth; it is said by the knowing ones of these parts that the more intelligent inhabitants of the Nubian Desert sometimes visit the Red Sea to enjoy its bracing climate—to them the Red Sea is the Skegness of the Tropics.

Pleasures there have been for us, of course; lazy days in the Mediterranean, when the sunshine has been friendly and the swimmers in the bathing-pool have splashed about, before stretching themselves luxuriously in the lovely slanting light of the late afternoon. Then the evenings.

First the sunsets, and the peacefulness that comes over the ship before dinner; people have retired to dress, and the solitary watcher, leaning on the ship's side, has the sense for a moment that he is being divested of personal identity and absorbed into the deepening beauty of the hour of twilight over the ocean as the evening star appears. At night the dancing begins, and here again it is good to escape from the glitter and animation, to withdraw and watch from a point apart. Then it is possible to feel the pathos of contrast —the light and happy intimacy of life brought together for a moment by chance; and the surrounding and lasting immensity of the Indian Ocean. And while all the laughter of young people goes on, and the elders sit domestically in lounge and drawing-room enjoying familiar comforts, the ship moves on, a beautiful sensitive creature, with the flexibility of a canoe and the power and grandeur of an ocean-going liner; through the night it moves, throbbing with a poised life of its own, making a wake in the water delicate as a chain. At the moment we are well beyond Aden, a sun-cursed pile of brown rock, oleaginous, with the refuse kites flapping in the air—a place where the White Man's Burden, and the Black Man's Burden too, can be felt as a weariness to flesh and spirit. We are following the track of a monsoon, and the ship is rolling. In the middle of the night it is thrilling for the landsman to listen from his cabin to the surge outside, and to feel the whole of the boat's nervous system working; you can hear the heart of it. I have grown to love the ship and the quiet certainty of the men who control its strength, grace, and nobility.

# CHAPTER IV

## GOOD-BYE TO THE *ORION*

*October* 17

NOT without mixed feelings did we come to the end of our voyage on October 13th, for, glad as we were to set foot in Australia, it was sad to say 'Good-bye' to the *Orion*. Life on a ship is concentrated in so small a space that in a month a man exceeds the common length of days. The distractions and responsibilities of the world come for a while to an end; as the hours go by we can almost count each pulsation of existence; consciousness and sense of personal identity become pure and absolute. And a strange sort of pathos falls on the little world we make for ourselves during the voyage; we know it cannot last long, that friendships almost certainly will come to an end soon, that all our efforts to reproduce the world we have left on land must end in irony—yet we do indeed reproduce it, I am afraid, with as many as possible of its foibles and pretensions. We live as though in a bubble which we have ourselves blown up, and as the voyage goes on the more does the bubble swell to bursting-point.

I have loved the evenings sitting in the 'Tavern' before dinner, watching the swimmers in the bathing-pool while the sun sank over the Indian Ocean and the sky turned to a sudden purple and stars appeared as though kindled one by one. I loved the careless fun of the games deck, the fun with the children in their own playground. I loved to go at half-past ten every morning into what I called the 'Market

Place', because it was there that C. B. Fry held court amongst the deck-chairs and the passing life of the ship; where we discussed all things under the sun. Perhaps our arguments were rather too contrapuntal to be easily followed by the listening throng; we each went our way, talking for art's sake, keeping count of our own bull's-eyes. But one day, just to tease him, I said: 'Well, Charles, good morning. No hemlock yet? Give us your views on the origin of the Iambic.' It was a pure piece of banter; the word 'Iambic' came to my mind by the merest chance. I might as well have asked him to explain the origin of King Cole or green cabbages. But Fry, without a moment's hesitation, launched into a remarkable piece of virtuoso exposition; in half an hour he sketched, with a swift touch and comprehensive illustrative detail, the history of prosody. And he had not finished when I left him and went for my morning walk seven times round the deck, making the mile. Each time I passed the ship's centre (the 'Market Place') he was still at it—'You see what I mean? However . . .' He wore a confusing variety of clothes day by day, clothes of strange dyes, patterns, and purposes. Only once did he appear (save at dinner) in tolerably reasonable guise, and that was at a fancy-dress ball, when he simulated an ascetic yet genial scoutmaster. The next day he wore what I called his deep-sea fishing attire, and I said: 'Glad to see you back in fancy dress, Charles'.

The team went quietly about their pleasures. Verity read *Seven Pillars of Wisdom* from beginning to end. Hammond won at all games, from chess to deck quoits. Maurice Leyland smoked his pipe, and Duckworth danced each evening with a nice understanding of what, socially, he was doing. Wyatt took many photographs and developed them himself. Fry, armed with a most complicated camera, also took many photographs, and none of them could be developed.

After we left Colombo the heat mercifully cooled down and a fresh wind blew. We came upon the Cocos Islands suddenly on a windy morning. Never shall I forget the romantic beauty of this experience. All the adventure stories of my youth sprang to life; here was Stevenson, Ballantyne, Defoe. On the little beach, silent and empty, there was surely Man Friday's footprint; the colours on the water evoked visions of enchanted lagoons, treasure, and coral. In a towering sea two little boats came bravely to take a barrel from the *Orion* containing the quarterly supply of rations for the handful of men who work on the islands, supporting the Empire and the White Man's Burden. The barrel was taken on board, and mighty waves swept past the two boats, sometimes hiding them from our view. On the *Orion* we all leaned over the side and waved farewell. And the last we saw of the little boats was their plungings and swayings as they returned to the island, with the men waving farewell in return; there was not a person on board the *Orion* who did not feel the emotion of the scene. 'It makes a lump come into your throat,' said William Voce of Nottinghamshire.

When we reached Fremantle it was seven in the morning. We had to be up and about early. Many times on the voyage I had wakened in the dawn and looked through my port-hole. There is magic in things seen from a ship's porthole; it becomes a magic mirror. I saw the sunrise on the Indian Ocean through my porthole, and felt ashamed to be prying into an act of beauty so secret and removed from human interference. Through my porthole I saw Australia for the first time.

# CHAPTER V

# PERTH

WE reached Fremantle on October 13th, and at the customs the officials were so keen to obtain our autographs that our baggage went through with commendable swiftness. I was not pleased with Fremantle, and I protested against the tradition which insists that every English cricket team should enter Australia by this door of bleak utility. We soon found out that Fremantle prepares, by contrast, an artful introduction to the country. We got into a car, and at once C. B. Fry began a far-reaching discourse on Australian architecture. Suddenly the scene changed as though a revolving stage had been turned round; we saw Perth in front of us, one of the prettiest cities in the world, surely, a city full of clear sunshine freshened by the river, a gleaming stretch of water along which I expected Lohengrin to appear at any moment on his white swan.

At Perth I saw my first Australian cricket pitch; it was being prepared, or manufactured, when we got to the ground. A friendly old horse named Jess pulled the roller; he wore shoes and walked with care. The groundsman was a perfect type, grizzled and in love with his work. The pitch astonished me, much though I had learned in the past about Australian pitches. It shimmered in the heat; I thought that if the Nelson monument had stood at one end, with a row of shops, I should have thought I was walking down the Strand. The important fact is that it did not play abnormally fast, though the Perth wicket is one of the fastest in the land. Australian pitches have changed in recent years; the old Bulli soil is no longer used. They tend to help spin bowlers after a day or two's usage; frequently they are the fast bowler's despair because of their want of fire. But they ask for leg-spin, propelled by considerable wrist energy. I shall make more of this important point. In the match against a combined 'Australian XI' at Perth, Badcock batted with the air of a master in the making: he hooked powerfully. We quickly realized that nearly all contemporary Australian batsmen employ the hook; yet before the English team was chosen, I heard statements in England that Gimblett was passed over because of his fondness for the hook. It was said that the stroke would be his undoing on the 'lightning' pitches of Australia. In the olden days Hirst and Jessop were both unable to hook there, but, as I say, the pace of the grounds has dwindled yards. If it is true that Gimblett's hook kept him out of the English team, here is another little irony. My impression, as the tour went on, is that Gimblett would have batted very much in the modern Australian fashion.

At Perth I played cricket for the first time for many years, actually bowled on Australian soil. It came about this way: some humorist conceived the idea of a match between the English journalists and the Australian journalists. And at first we liked the idea. We agreed to practise, or rather, as I put it to William Pollock, we agreed to have a net to find out whether it would be wise to have a net. After one or two arduous experiments we unanimously decided not to practise, and the match was mercifully cancelled. Arthur Mailey took us through our trials and turned the ball a yard. I could turn from the off only half an inch. Crude though our efforts were, the lesson learned helped me to understand later on why Fleetwood-Smith spun the ball dangerously at Adelaide and why Verity did not.

Mere finger spin is next to useless in Australia in dry weather.

At our net practice dear old Harry Carson did an extraordinary thing. This delightful companion, with his much-admired grey hair and aristocratic stoop, decided to bowl. He once was a cricketer of talent, but the years tell on a man. With difficulty and several explanatory 'Don'tcher knows', he got his arm over somehow and struck the wing net with the ball. At last he achieved a deadly, because surprising, straightness which almost overwhelmed Pollock, who was the batsman; Pollock had to play with a severely straight bat, at least so he told us. The fact is nobody saw what he did, for while Carson for once avoided hitting the net with the ball he himself personally hit the net; he crossed his feet, reeled backwards clutching at the air, murmured 'Don'tcher know', then fell helpless as a landed fish, and was caught into the meshes of the net, where his trouser buttons became entangled. We cut him out after we had risen from the ground on which we had all collapsed, helpless with laughter. Even Arthur Mailey's inscrutable face flickered. As I say, nobody saw Pollock's masterly defence against Carson's straight high dropping ball.

Perth gave us twelve happy days. Every night we were taken somewhere to dinner; an association of Commercial Travellers made speeches at us, scores of them, with references to the 'Festive Board'. And they sang at us 'Why were they born to be-yootiful; why were they born at all?' This dinner ended in an orgy of song; I conducted (with a control and eloquence that astonished me) the 'Lily of Laguna', 'Little Dolly Daydream', all the dear old airs of Leslie Stuart and Eugene Stratton. The singers, including Charles Fry, followed my beat and gestures with feeling and responsive musicianship—now a crescendo, then, at a sudden and Toscanini-like admonishment, a decrescendo which almost faded into silence. I have seldom seen so many happy men in my life, all of us making glorious fools of ourselves. I nearly ripped one of Pollock's eyes with the fish-knife I used as a baton. The 'Lily of Laguna' was so successfully received that by request it was repeated by a carefully chosen octet, including, of course, Charles Fry, who chose himself. They stood in a row a yard in front of me at the top of the table. To my dying day I shall see their faces, strained to attention, awaiting my first beat, arms by the side, like a lot of nervous schoolboys. The harmonies were excellent, in spite of the fact that Fry sang the wrong tune. He sang 'Little Dolly Daydream' throughout.

This was not the only music I heard in Perth; I heard more good music in Perth than in any other place during the tour. I was invited to houses in Cottesloe, a gracious residential district up the hill. I actually heard songs by Hugo Wolf, sung intelligently and well. Perth is so far away from the rest of the world that it has to make its own life. The people are unlike average Australians; they speak Kensington English, the women dress with refinement in and out of doors. Even many of the men dress well. Perth has to live without Test match cricket because of its isolation. The deprivation has its consolation; there is too much time and talk devoted to cricket or other sports in the larger capitals. Melbourne is supposed to be Australia's most cultured city; I doubt if it is more civilized than Perth, allowing for differences in population. Certainly it is not more homely, pleasant, or good to see. We left Perth sadly, and began the long railway journey over the desert, nearly 2000 miles, in a train strictly given to temperance.

During the journey we passed at long intervals little shacks or gatherings of homesteads. Hands were waved at us, and wistfully our train was watched until we disappeared in the vast waste. One evening we stopped to take in water; there in the sunset we saw a cricket pitch, built out of railway sleepers. The falling light glinted on the sand, which stretched away on every side; in the silence our voices seemed loud and vulgar. A few tin sheds explained the presence of the wooden cricket pitch: a sad, lonely tribute to the game's hold over Australia. No wonder they can beat our best, with a team chosen from a population not as large as London's.

# CHAPTER VI

# COMING TO GRIPS

THE journey of the team from Perth, through Adelaide and Melbourne to Sydney, was, from the view of cricket, depressing. We needed all the hospitality of Australia to cheer us up during a period in which England's batsmen seemed ready to double-up and become congested at the first sight of a slow leg-spin bowler, whatever his name— Mudge, Sludge, Gregory, Fredericks, Stoakes, Styles, or Thompson. Even Hammond, in spite of four consecutive hundreds, allowed a leg-stump attack to keep him more or less passive; throughout the rubber the Australians exploited to useful ends the theory that Hammond cannot play match-winning strokes if the ball is kept away from his off stump. For years I have watched Hammond crashing four after four through the covers, off English bowlers who as a class have not yet found out (what the Australians quickly found out) that Hammond is weak on the on-side.

In November, 1936, I saw for the first time Adelaide Oval and the cathedral steeples outside. I walked to the ground along an avenue which made me instinctively look for Carlton House Terrace on the right, for on the left was surely St. James's Park. The approach to the Adelaide Oval is as beautiful as the Oval itself. As I walked through the gardens on a hot morning, a bee hummed in the heat, and suddenly a number of men appeared from nowhere, removed their coats, waistcoats, and watch-chains, sat down on camp-stools in the shade, produced trumpets and trombones, and proceeded to play the Egmont overture of Beethoven. A surprising spectacle on the morning of a cricket match at Adelaide between England and South Australia.

The Oval is the prettiest of the world's big cricket grounds. It is green and spacious; the hills in the background seem not far away. Australian cricket grounds are usually amphitheatrical; Sydney and Melbourne are hard and efficient erections in concrete; the Hill at Sydney disappointed me when first I saw it—a pleasant green bank on which the wild thyme might easily blow. The big Mound at Sheffield is much more forbidding and vociferous; but of course on this tour the 'Hill' was on probation, so to say; politeness was indirectly encouraged by the police. Melbourne is the biggest of the Australian fields; it is a stadium. There is sign of 'big business' everywhere. The lounge at the top of the members' enclosure is opulent; few edifices could hope to show a larger splendour, though probably there is something approaching it in Buckingham Palace. Vast crowds assemble at Test matches in Melbourne; the whole city gives up work for the occasion. Women are as numerous almost as men, and they scream all day long. More of these matters later; but a Test match in England, compared with a Test match in Australia, is mild and local. Everybody talks cricket, as I say, perpetually. During one of the Test matches of the tour, it was necessary that a meeting of important statesmen should be held one morning at Canberra; a radio was put into the council room, and the Prime Minister interpolated his remarks on policy with 'Another four for Bradman'. While we were at Adelaide on our first visit in November, one's telephone began to ring at seven in the morning—invitations to speak at cricket lunches, or to visit schools and talk cricket to the boys, or invitations to houses in the country for the week-end. A little girl came twenty miles just to obtain the English team's autographs; she brought flowers which turned my room into a prima donna's dressing-room after a first night. It was the same at Christmas at Usher's in Sydney; perfect strangers sent roses, cigarettes, chocolates, Christmas greetings. The Australians are the kindest people I have ever known. It was at Melbourne that a cinema company asked if they could 'film' me. I agreed for fun. It was to take the form of an interview. One of the questions put to me was: 'And what would your age be, Mr. Cardus, when you first saw Victor Trumper?' My reply was: 'That is not a fair question to put to a "movie" star.' The film cut out this wit and gave me an American accent instead. I bowled at the nets at one or two schools in Adelaide and Perth. And I saw the way the Australians catch them young. The practices were grimly conducted. No foolery, no shouts of 'Heads! Heads!' such as we hear in nets at an English school; no waste of energy, no flippancy about 'four to get and the last man in'. Every boy batted and bowled with visions of Test match honours palpably before him. Googly bowling was plentiful, and the wickets were perfect. Even in the parks, where the poorest boys play, there is a chance to learn scientific cricket on the pre-pared concrete pitches. Cricket in Australia is a religion, and almost an affair of national control. The Grades relate the most modest team to the Australian team itself. Ability can move up, through the various Grades of each club; nothing is out of sight, so to say. The Grades are the rung on the international ladder. I sometimes felt that the whole country was an arsenal of cricket, with the women, as well as the men, under conscription.

# CHAPTER VII

# BOILING POINT

THE first days in Sydney were troublous: New South Wales won, and only time saved the match against an 'Australian XI'—Voce and Leyland were defending at the end, last men in. Leyland skilfully took the bowling (or 'strike') for several trying minutes; he calculated, exactly, which would be the day's last over but one; he played each ball safely away for nothing, confident he could get a single from the eighth ball. And after the sixth ball the umpire walked to square-leg. 'Hey, lad,' cried Leyland after him, 'wheer's t' a goain'?' But the umpire only indicated that it was 'over'. Leyland surveyed the changing field, then said to Oldfield: 'By gum, the ——'s done me.'

The poor form up to December hindered our enjoyment for a while of Sydney, even of the oysters at Usher's, and of the city's mild flavour of New York at night, with its neon signs. But nothing could spoil the spell which fell upon the harbour, which, I think, is one of the few underrated famous places of the earth. I could live at Vaucluse or Watson's Bay and be happy, given a gramophone and Test matches only once every four years.

Australians were as much concerned as the rest of us at England's form when the seven-hundred-mile journey to Brisbane was begun at the end of November. There were even rumours about that Allen and his men were deliberately playing at half pressure, just for deception. Even against Queensland, England collapsed on the first day, and once again a slow bowler caused the breakdown, a

33

mute inglorious leg-breaker named Allen; nay, he did not bowl leg-break, but 'donkey drops'. Magnificent hitting by Barnett cleared the air a little in time for the beginning of the first Test match at Woolloongabba.

Woolloongabba is the name of the district at Brisbane where Test matches are played; it is a remote spot to an Englishman. When I contemplated Woolloongabba, with its corrugated iron and bits of rope and its wooden benches, and when the uproar of the crowd began and I saw in the crowd men bleached with sun and garbed in rough habiliments, I thought to myself, 'This is cricket in Bret Harte's Roaring Camp'. And I expected the arrival of Tom Mix and the Sheriff at any moment. But for all its lack of Melbourne's, Adelaide's, and Sydney's organization, we came to like Woolloongabba; we certainly lost our misgivings about Brisbane. And I confess that to begin with Brisbane rather scared me, in spite of everybody's friendliness and kindness. You see, it was my first taste of a sub-tropical place. I had never before seen a mosquito net, and the shroud of it filled me with a curious creepy feeling as I surveyed it, on a steaming night in my bedroom at the Queensland Club. I had come in from a walk, along a road thick with nocturnal heat; crickets chirped and winged things hit me in the face. The Queensland Club was a hostel, a refuge from alien darkness. Then I saw the mosquito net. But as soon as I climbed under it I felt a curious charm; I thrilled once more with the romantic sense of being a boy under a tent, hidden away, enjoying a secret pleasure. Then I slept—for an hour or two. In five nights at Brisbane I slept five hours. The dawns woke me; I began to hate the sun as it came up every morning, a lidless eye. The birds in the botanical garden opposite my bedroom emitted piercing noises; my God, I felt, how far away I am from all familiar things! This was a provincial Englishman's exaggeration, of course; Brisbane is not one of Australia's fastnesses; there are beautiful buildings in the city, and I met there people whom I shall hope to have as friends for the rest of my life.

I imagine it was at Woolloongabba that Mr. Micawber settled; and probably Mrs. Jellyby's gaze embraced it. I do not speak unkindly, I hope, of Brisbane; only in Perth did we feel as much warmth of heart as here. I wish only to set the matches in the scene as I saw and lived it; and it takes all sorts to make a world, certainly to make Australia, which has not yet come under the standardizing inhibitions of an over-sophisticated civilization.

To everybody's amazement, England won at Brisbane. Rain after the fifth day helped Allen to clinch an issue which, as I have already said, was settled by straight cricket in conditions even to both sides. Bradman failed because the ball flew a little; at Sydney he failed likewise. He failed at Lord's in 1934, against Verity on a bowler's pitch—and what an inglorious failure that one was! Until Bradman plays a great innings against a flying and spitting ball we cannot put him into Victor Trumper's class. On good wickets he is the most commanding, the safest, and most prolific batsman the game has ever known.

I did not believe in his failures on the good wickets at Brisbane, Sydney, and Melbourne; when I saw him turn a ball round to leg from Verity straight into Robins's hands on New Year's Day, I was terrified. He had, in the second innings at Sydney, a few days before, been bowled by a prodigious long-hop from Verity. The suspicious thing was that he was not being technically bowled; some knot in his own psychology was troubling him. I remembered how in 1934, in England, he found mastery at the critical moment at Leeds, when Australia had lost three wickets for thirty-nine. Up to that time Bradman had been in a sad state. And now, as then, he won the rubber at the challenging point. There is no doubt that he turned the scale, after England had won two out of two, while Bradman was failing. He was not a fit man at Brisbane. And critics were suggesting that he could not combine captaincy with double-centuries. At Adelaide in November he told me he did not wish any more to pile up vast scores. He certainly batted at Brisbane, in the first innings, with something of the jazzed energy he showed us in England during the first two Test matches of 1934. It was at Brisbane, I fancy, that Allen first decided to set a more or less protective field for Bradman, with the idea of blocking his strokes and in the hope that Bradman would be driven to recklessness. The plan seemed to work for a while, but in the end it proved, I am sure, Allen's undoing. More of that later; let us at last arrive at, or get to grips with, the first Test match.

# CHAPTER VIII

# FIRST TEST—BRISBANE

*November 27—December 2, 1936 .*

## FIRST DAY

### ENGLAND First Innings

| | | | |
|---|---|---|---:|
| Worthington, c. Oldfield, b. McCormick | . | . | 0 |
| Barnett, c. Oldfield, b. O'Reilly | . | . | 69 |
| Fagg, c. Oldfield, b. McCormick | . | . | 4 |
| Hammond, c. Robinson, b. McCormick | . | . | 0 |
| Leyland, b. Ward | . | . | 126 |
| Ames, c. Chipperfield, b. Ward . | . | . | 24 |
| Hardstaff, not out | . | . | 27 |
| R. W. V. Robins, not out | . | . | 6 |
| Extras (b. 1, l.b. 3 n.b. 3) . | . | . | 7 |
| Total (for 6 wickets) . | . | . | 263 |

To bat.—G. O. Allen, Verity, and Voce.

Fall of the wickets:

| 1 | 2 | 3 | 4 | 5 | 6 |
|---|---|---|---|---|---|
| 0 | 20 | 20 | 119 | 162 | 252 |

ALLEN and Bradman came forth at noon to toss, and Allen won, and the storm-clouds went by, and the crowd simmered, and before the action began they stood up and examined the Press as though we were demented caged animals, which probably we were. Rumour, with a thousand tongues and typewriters, strode the blast. A slight dust storm added to the general sense of impending misery.

The beginning was catastrophic; McCormick's first ball, which he bowled like a hurricane, pitched short, and rose high at Worthington's left shoulder. Worthington hooked impulsively, foozled his stroke, skied it, and Oldfield, after starting late, ran forward in a panic, and held the catch. Poor Worthington stood dazed a moment, then departed head down.

In the same over, McCormick struck Fagg in the middle of the body, and the crowd's noise ceased while Fagg retired for repairs. McCormick's next ball rose near Fagg's cranium; we could see for ourselves that McCormick's two short legs were not merely decorative. But soon one of them was moved to the slips, and the rising angle of the attack became more in accordance with the modern batsman's view of respectable fast bowling. In quick sequence Barnett cut McCormick for four, edged him dangerously for four, and cut him again with a hammer-swing right from the shoulders. Sievers at the other end kept a length, and once or twice a late swinger heated Fagg's brow.

The game momentarily quietened, but, ah, the crafty way the great game prepares its ironies! Fagg tried a leg glance against McCormick, and Oldfield caught him with the most lovely sideways swoop. Then Hammond perished first ball to the sound of widespread approval; McCormick sent him one just short of a length, and it rose above Hammond's left hip at an acute angle. Hammond contorted himself, stabbed with sudden reluctance, trying to get the ball away to the on somewhere and somehow. He spooned it up horribly, and silly short leg had no alternative but to hold a catch which, in its helplessness, saw Hammond a sad, dispossessed monarch. McCormick bowled with hostile aim, at the pace which compels the hurried irrational stroke. For half an hour he is easily the fastest bowler of the present day. While the ball was new he cleverly varied his attack on the leg stump to a danger zone outside the off stump. Now and again he inserted a 'kicker'. His length was not, so far as I could see, shorter than his pace warranted.

Leyland walked in with his long arms and an inexpressive face and joined Barnett; and O'Reilly lumbered into the fary, wheeling his arms heavily; and Ward came on. Ward's first over was a clever variation on the theme of a googly. Barnett played it with his bat a closely padlocked door, while Leyland looked on, still unemotional, if not unconcerned.

The struggle could be felt intensely, a grand bone of contention was being gnawed by the various dogs. But Barnett was cool and brave, and though Leyland could not do as he wished, the England temperature eased a little. In fact, a massive off-drive for six by Barnett from Ward let a momentary breeze blow. He hit the next ball for four arrogantly, in the manner of a man in a beleaguered city attempting a sortie. Barnett was admirable, but the batting still needed certainty of touch. I felt that both Leyland and Barnett were often obliged to play strokes which the bowlers wanted them to make, but which they themselves would rather have evaded. Still, no further disaster occurred before 1.30 when the cricketers came in to lunch, to recover from a scalding morning's work.

After lunch, Ward bowled at the Pavilion end, and Leyland sent a high chance to McCormick at mid-on. The Australian fielding was only good; I did not feel always that organized hostility with every man shooting rays of menace at the batsmen from all over the field. Barnett went his stylish, confident way, making strokes strong and handsome. I particularly liked his cool treatment of Ward's spin. He waited for it, which was often easy for him to do, since Ward tended to pitch a shade short. O'Reilly seemed industrious this time, rather than creative. The game's balance became more nicely poised, though England's track was still long and uphill. None the less, the cricket of Barnett suggested that a standard-bearer had seized the bullet-ridden England colours, and was determined to keep them aloft. And Leyland was his soldier-at-arms, hard pressed now and then, maybe, but shrewd and full of horse sense.

Leyland was again missed, to his quiet and not stressed satisfaction—this time in the slips off McCormick, his score in the twenties. The Australians were not putting forward their traditional ruthlessness, not keeping the enemy down once they were down. As a fact, the next advance of Australia occurred because of one of those mistakes which only batsmen make who are in form; Barnett sought to turn a quickish ball by O'Reilly to leg and was caught by the matchless Oldfield. Ranjitsinhji wrote an illuminating passage once, demonstrating how it needs a fine eye and a good player to get caught at the wicket in the way Barnett was caught. Barnett's cricket throughout appealed to the imagination, and to our sense of cricket's art. Occasionally he wavered before the good length spin, but, as I have hinted, the spin did not consistently pitch on the blind spot.

The wine of a wicket made O'Reilly's tail temporarily stand up, and he nearly overwhelmed Ames' first ball, leg before, and, judging from Oldfield's leap forward, caught at the wicket simultaneously, from a 'heaven help me' push at a most bad-tempered delivery. The weather cooled, but the electricity remained in the game, though I did not always feel the Australian bowlers were as aggressive as they were trying to look, after the morning's taste of blood. Sievers is only an honest effort by Nature to repeat Alan Fairfax; and she never even tries to repeat a masterpiece—she breaks the mould in which a Trumble or a Turner is fashioned.

An immense amount of smoke was wafted over the field,

and I dreamed of Bramall Lane, where, from the pavilion, you can count twenty chimneys. Leyland, perhaps, felt at home, for he reached 50. It was not a characteristic performance, though, until later in the day. Australia were most unlucky to lose the aid of McCormick, who, they tell me, suddenly became afflicted with lumbago. In Manchester it takes me, and most of us, in the small of the back regularly, but then Manchester is, as everybody knows, Manchester. Tea obviously refreshed the bowlers, for at once Ward spun a ball from leg at the well-flighted length he should always try to bowl. Ames felt for it, and died the logical death—caught in the slips. Hardstaff had to come in against slow spin. How he survived at all was hard to say. I was reminded of the lady at the fair who has knives thrown all round her body, and escapes hurt. Leyland nursed him, but Leyland was once more badly missed, now at 71, from a return to Ward. The cricket was not hereabout good enough for a Test match. It needed more class and personality. But Leyland persisted, and conquered by his rare character. Hardstaff somehow resurrected himself gradually, and his innings had a kind of second birth; anyhow, he stayed in. Meanwhile, Leyland reached his century, and thrived on his work as it went on.

He and Barnett bailed the water out of the almost capsized boat, and when he fell five minutes from the close of play, even Huddersfield or Pudsey could not have given him a warmer ovation back to the pavilion than the one he got at Brisbane.

## SECOND DAY

ENGLAND First Innings

| | | |
|---|---|---|
| Worthington, c. Oldfield, b. McCormick | . . | 0 |
| Barnett, c. Oldfield, b. O'Reilly | . . | 69 |
| Fagg, c. Oldfield, b. McCormick | . . | 4 |

ENGLAND First Innings—*continued*

| | |
|---|---:|
| Hammond, c. Robinson, b. McCormick . . | o |
| Leyland, b. Ward . . . . . . | 126 |
| Ames, c. Chipperfield, b. Ward . . . | 24 |
| Hardstaff, c. McCabe, b. O'Reilly . . | 43 |
| R. W. V. Robins, c. sub. (Brown), b. O'Reilly . | 38 |
| G. O. Allen, c. McCabe, b. O'Reilly . . | 35 |
| Verity, c. Sievers, b. O'Reilly . . . | 7 |
| Voce, not out . . . . . . | 4 |
| Extras (b. 1, l.b. 3, n.b. 4) . . . | 8 |
| | |
| Total . . . . . . | 358 |

England first-innings bowling analysis

| | O. | M. | R. | W. |
|---|---:|---:|---:|---:|
| McCormick . . | 8 | 1 | 26 | 3 |
| Sievers . . . | 16 | 5 | 42 | 0 |
| O'Reilly . . | 40·6 | 13 | 102 | 5 |
| Ward . . . | 36 | 3 | 138 | 2 |
| Chipperfield . . | 11 | 3 | 32 | 0 |
| McCabe. . . | 2 | 0 | 10 | 0 |

Fall of the wickets:

| 1 | 2 | 3 | 4 | 5 | 6 | 7 | 8 | 9 | 10 |
|---|---|---|---|---|---|---|---|---|---|
| 0 | 20 | 20 | 119 | 162 | 252 | 311 | 311 | 343 | 358 |

AUSTRALIA First Innings

| | |
|---|---:|
| J. H. Fingleton, not out . . . . | 61 |
| C. L. Badcock, b. Allen . . . . | 8 |
| D. G. Bradman, c. Worthington, b. Voce . . | 38 |
| S. J. McCabe, not out . . . . | 37 |
| Extras . . . . . . | 7 |
| | |
| Total (for 2 wickets) . . . . | 151 |

To bat.—A. G. Chipperfield, R. Robinson, W. A. Oldfield, W. J. O'Reilly, M. Sievers, F. Ward, E. L. McCormick.

Fall of the wickets:

| 1 | 2 |
|---|---|
| 13 | 89 |

There was a congested crowd when, at high noon, the umpires attended to the stumps and fixed them like students of trigonometry. The pitch looked like a Roman pavement discovered by antiquarians, or a grave or historic barrow containing the honourable bones of departed and disillusioned bowlers. The day's first ball from Ward was cut for four by Robins; he cut it when it was about to bounce for the second but by no means the last time. Then in O'Reilly's opening over three boundaries occurred, an exquisite leg glance and a dangerous pull by Hardstaff, and a glorious leg glance by Robins. The attack was here-about disreputable, and Hardstaff twice drove Ward to the off in his happiest Trent Bridge vein. Robins was as good as Hardstaff, nimble of feet, cutting with a terrier alacrity and with a beauty of rhythm in his cover-drive. In half an hour Robins and Hardstaff scored 40, and struck a note of happy, easeful challenge which was new to an England innings this tour.

Hardstaff was caught from an effort to sweep O'Reilly to leg; even the gesture of the stroke told us that Hardstaff was escaping from the complicated interstices of self-doubt. Robins fell to a catch on the off-side soon after Hardstaff had departed, from a bad shot under the ball, but again I liked the offensive gesture. O'Reilly's tail stood up visibly again. On Friday it was as low to the ground as that of a dog who had been severely reprimanded.

Allen and Verity proceeded to hold up the advancing enemy; Verity was very studious as he attended to O'Reilly's changes of pace, solving them like a sixth-form mathematician, if sometimes counting on his fingers surreptitiously. Allen tried to drive, but could not quite time his strokes; still, he stayed in, and Verity would not get out, and once again I felt some weakness of penetration in the Australian forces.

The ground was packed after lunch, and one man sat on an adjacent roof and watched the play for nothing. Verity at length decided to hit O'Reilly to leg, and was caught square; something had to be done, I suppose, for the game

was becoming static, yet I fancy that Emmott Robinson
would have asked Verity what he imagined he was doing,
and whether he thought he was playing in a cricket match.
With Voce in last, Allen ran out and smote O'Reilly for
four, and a straight six, and died fighting, caught superbly
at mid-on by McCabe from another damn-the-con-
sequences gesture. It took Australia nearly an hour to
capture England's last two wickets, which fell to O'Reilly,
and lent a gentle touch of polish to the great bowler's
analysis. So concluded the drama's first act, and during the
interval part of the crowd had another opportunity to
inspect the Press box.

In a violent atmosphere, Australia's innings began. The
roars were colossal when Badcock at once drove Allen
straight for three and pulled him for four. And when
suddenly Badcock played on by pulling his stroke askew
in a back defensive effort, the sky was split by the noise;
it was gladiatorial; I expected the lions and the Christians.

Bradman was heralded with trumpets and trombones of
acclamation as he walked to the wicket, and the whole of
the multitude's orchestra crashed out as he cut Allen for
four and pulled him gigantically for four. Then Voce
missed the edge of Bradman's bat by a hair's-breadth and
hysteria let out its shriek; it was a lucky escape. But
heavens! what a game this cricket is in Australia, what a
battleground, not to say a shambles, is made of a cricket
field; how I shall greet the green peacefulness next year of
Worcester and Horsham. I love the grandeur of Test
matches in Australia, the strain and the power, but I am a
man of peace, and this is war.

Allen rested after a few overs, in which he seemed not
only willing but anxious to break his back for the cause.
Hammond relieved him, and the tension eased, though

Fingleton once or twice rekindled panic by a hesitant slip stroke. Bradman missed one or two, but I felt the wonderful engine of his technique at work; the dynamo was throbbing, in spite of a fortunate slice through the slips off Allen when he was 21. Bradman often begins against fast bowling as though some deep periodic law of fallibility were working in him, making him one of the human family. His genius has its own logic and authority; apparently he is free to play off any foot, and to transform into greatness and grandeur what in other players would be error fatal and unlovely. There is the *gamin* about him somewhere. Fingleton defended stoutly, a worthy anonymous helpmate to the darling and paragon of the crowd.

Though Allen bowled with heroic intent, he was expensive, and Verity came on, secret and self-contained as an oyster; his bowling looked amiable on the flawless wicket, but it contained an inward obliquity; the words of his mouth were smoother than butter, but war was in his heart. He lured Bradman into second thoughts, and at once he insulted the great man by placing a silly point. At tea Bradman had not reached 50; Verity skilfully put him on a leash. Verity did not directly capture Bradman's wicket, but he contributed to the downfall, which came so suddenly after tea that the crowd was shocked. Voce sent an outswinger which Bradman seemed to try to force backfooted to the off; the ball veered to the slips, and Worthington pounced on it. Verity had brought a more healthy atmosphere for England into the game before tea; a silly point to Bradman spoke volumes of moral ascendancy. After his rhetorical beginning against Allen, Bradman lost something of his power; he was not hitting as hard as he did when first I saw him in England six years ago—at least, not yet.

Fingleton was always doing good by stealth, observed

by the scorers, if not always by the rest of us. Even McCabe could not attack; Verity's length checked many of his drives, changing them to pushes.

And so the even day proceeded to its close. Suddenly Voce pitched one short, and McCabe swung terrifically at it and lofted it high over mid-on, and the crowd roared and screamed as Barnett turned to chase it; but vain was his dive along the grass, for he missed it by inches. The roaring and screaming subsided, and when the stumps were drawn everybody departed, and the sun went suddenly down, and the lovely velvet of a Brisbane twilight concealed the battlefield.

---

### THIRD DAY

#### ENGLAND First Innings

| | |
|---|---:|
| Worthington, c. Oldfield, b. McCormick . . | 0 |
| Barnett, c. Oldfield, b. O'Reilly . . . | 69 |
| Fagg, c. Oldfield, b. McCormick . . | 4 |
| Hammond, c. Robinson, b. McCormick . . | 0 |
| Leyland, b. Ward . . . . . . | 126 |
| Ames, c. Chipperfield, b. Ward . . . | 24 |
| Hardstaff, c. McCabe, b. O'Reilly . . | 43 |
| R. W. V. Robins, c. sub. (Brown), b. O'Reilly . | 38 |
| G. O. Allen, c. McCabe, b. O'Reilly . . | 35 |
| Verity, c. Sievers, b. O'Reilly . . . | 7 |
| Voce, not out . . . . . . | 4 |
| Extras (b. 1, l.b. 3, n.b. 4) . . . | 8 |
| Total . . . . . | 358 |

England first-innings bowling analysis

| | O. | M. | R. | W. |
|---|---|---|---|---|
| McCormick . . | 8 | 1 | 26 | 3 |
| Sievers . . . | 16 | 5 | 42 | 0 |
| O'Reilly . . | 40·6 | 13 | 102 | 5 |
| Ward . . . | 36 | 3 | 138 | 2 |
| Chipperfield . . | 11 | 3 | 32 | 0 |
| McCabe . . | 2 | 0 | 10 | 0 |

Fall of the wickets:

| 1 | 2 | 3 | 4 | 5 | 6 | 7 | 8 | 9 | 10 |
|---|---|---|---|---|---|---|---|---|----|
| 0 | 20 | 20 | 119 | 162 | 252 | 311 | 311 | 343 | 358 |

## AUSTRALIA First Innings

| | |
|---|---:|
| J. H. Fingleton, b. Verity . . . . | . 100 |
| C. L. Badcock, b. Allen . . . . | . 8 |
| D. G. Bradman, c. Worthington, b. Voce . | . 38 |
| S. J. McCabe, c. Barnett, b. Voce . | . 51 |
| R. Robinson, c. Hammond, b. Voce . | . 2 |
| A. G. Chipperfield, c. Ames, b. Voce . | . 7 |
| M. Sievers, b. Allen . . . . | . 8 |
| W. A. Oldfield, c. Ames, b. Voce . | . 6 |
| W. J. O'Reilly, c. Leyland, b. Voce . | . 3 |
| F. Ward, c. Hardstaff, b. Allen . . | . 0 |
| E. L. McCormick, not out . . . | . 1 |
| Extras (b. 4, l.b. 1, n.b. 5) . . . | . 10 |
| Total . . . . . | . 234 |

Australia first-innings bowling analysis

| | O. | M. | R. | W. |
|---|---|---|---|---|
| Allen . . . | 16 | 2 | 71 | 3 |
| Voce . . . | 20·6 | 5 | 41 | 6 |
| Hammond . . | 4 | 0 | 12 | 0 |
| Verity . . . | 28 | 11 | 52 | 1 |
| Robins . . . | 17 | 0 | 48 | 0 |

Fall of the wickets:

| 1 | 2 | 3 | 4 | 5 | 6 | 7 | 8 | 9 | 10 |
|---|---|---|---|---|---|---|---|---|----|
| 13 | 89 | 166 | 176 | 202 | 220 | 229 | 231 | 231 | 234 |

## ENGLAND Second Innings

| | |
|---|---:|
| Worthington, st. Oldfield, b. McCabe. | . 8 |
| Barnett, c. Badcock, b. Ward . . | . 26 |
| Fagg, not out . . . . . | . 24 |
| Hammond, not out . . . . | . 12 |
| Extras . . . . . | . 5 |
| Total (for 2 wickets) . . . | . 75 |

Fall of the wickets:

| 1 | 2 |
|---|---|
| 17 | 50 |

With every need at the day's outset to keep the situation tense and the net taut round McCabe and Fingleton, Allen daringly put Robins on as one of his opening bowlers. He himself attacked from the pavilion end. Robins is liable to bowl long-hops, but on this occasion he got the ball three parts the way of its journey before pitching it. The length struck terror in my heart, all the same. I expected boundaries each ball. Allen himself was erratic, and McCabe drove him straight and cut him swift and in his best style. Too soon, from England's point of view, were the batsmen off the mark. Allen obviously shared the same idea, for he retired in favour of Voce, who at once put England ahead by keen bowling to the off side, beautiful in length, with only Allen at short leg. McCabe sought to hook a short one, and Barnett caught him at deep mid-on. A trap, surely, for McCabe on Saturday was warned with a dream book's precision of how he would lose his wicket to a dark, handsome man, which is a reasonably good description of Voce.

Fingleton hit Robins to the off, a grand shot with the back foot the propeller, and he pulled Robins rather rhetorically past Worthington at forward mid-on, but Voce's next over saw the passing of Robinson, who sightlessly put out his bat to a rare outswinger and sent a low catch as close to the ground almost as a swallow skimming water. Hammond took it with marvellous ease and grace at fine slip. At first Robinson did not realize he was out, and there was a polite pause. Presumably he received sentence on an appeal. Thus the wheel of the match once more swung England's way. Fingleton was the Australian hope now, with his bat straight and immobile, his mind cool and protective, looking inwards.

Allen's captaincy became interesting. Robins did not let

him down (helped by the fact that neither Fingleton nor Chipperfield is an expert at the cut), and he took off Voce, changed Robins over, and at the other end relied on Verity. The basic principle of the move was, we thought, a rest for Voce before the new ball was used at the two hundred. Verity's silly point and silly mid-on were so close to the block-hole that I half expected to see one of them obstruct the ball's flight. It was a spectacle which would have goaded Charles Macartney to acts of disruption, turning him livid with rage. A stranger coming into the ground would have been excused if he had thought Australia's two last men were in, with six runs needed for victory, in a match without a time limit. Robins found a nicely arched length in one over to Fingleton, and came terribly close to ensnaring him leg before. The umpire had to bend low and look hard and work out some mental geometry before he could decide in the batsman's favour. Then Chipperfield sent a dangerous hit from Robins to Allen on the off. The batting was so irresolute that I thought the silly point and silly mid-on were too deep. On the stroke of lunch, Voce again achieved a magnificent offside ball, and Chipperfield snicked it fatally without wishing to have anything to do with it. Allen baffled us because he did not claim the new ball for the rested and match-winning Voce. In fact, after two overs he took Voce off and trusted to Robins and Verity, a dangerously experimental procedure, in spite of one ball by Verity which spun and jumped delightfully and significantly. At a quarter to three, Fingleton turned Robins to the on for a single and reached his century, a worthy crown for hours of patient, devoted batting, all for his side, never showy or vain, but sheer steadfastness and shrewd skill; not a picture innings—an innings for the accountancy of cricket rather than for the art of the game, none the less an innings to be proud of, a conquest by character as well as by craft. Fingleton had no sooner acknowledged the crowd's applause than he was bowled by Verity. The ball came with Verity's arm and kept low. Allen's luck was with him— deeds are better than abstract theory.

I must confess that I was astonished at the Australian batting against the slow bowling. Voce's attack obviously commanded severe watchfulness, but on a hard ground Verity was allowed to bowl six consecutive maidens, and Robins at the other end was as suspiciously regarded. Both these bowlers were skilful, but they were allowed to display their arts at will: few, if any, efforts were made to hit them in front of the wicket. Robins, who would be the first to agree that he is no length bowler, could afford to leave his field vacant behind him.

Sievers defended well enough, but you can tell his period —post-war. Oldfield for a while stemmed the Australian landslide with Sievers until he fell another victim to Voce's quick outswinger. Then Sievers was bowled by Allen, playing very late, so late that the stroke was almost in time for next innings. Ward made reflex action at Allen, and Hardstaff caught him at silly mid-on, falling over to take a chance not hit far enough for him to reach without an effort. It was necessary for McCormick to come in with a runner, whose services were not elaborately wanted, for O'Reilly hopelessly pushed a catch to Leyland, who also had to roll and reach. Thus ended the sad and surprising tale of woe. Eight wickets fell for 83 in nearly three hours.

The England eleven were, as the man in Charles Dickens says, transmogrified: it was a hostile band of marauders. Voce was superb: no short stuff, no modern theories, but

correct length, much pace off the pitch, and the deadly
ball that leaves the bat just a little. Verity and Robins
jumped to their chances and performed a bluff sweet
enough to make the pavilion cat laugh. It seemed all too
good to be true—or too bad, according to one's point of
vision. As the Australian innings subsided, in the company
of a crowd that had been so happy and trusting, and was
now so sad, I thought of a passage in the diary of Samuel
Pepys: 'I went to Charing Cross to see Major-General
Harrison hanged, drawn, and quartered, which was done
there, he looking as cheerful as any man could do in that
condition.'

England's second innings began with the confidence
which confidence begets, until Worthington seemed to
become stumped off the wicket-keeper's boots. The occurrence escaped the eternal vigilance of the Press box: none
of us knew exactly how Worthington had got out. The
main thing was that he was out. The battle was bitter. The
Australian fielding shot out the old fierce opportunism.
O'Reilly bowled with all his strength and skill. The
Australians were fighting to redeem an evil day. Every
ball bowled was a challenge; we could feel at the edge of
the field the strain and ordeal through which the players
were passing. Twice was Barnett beaten, once by Ward,
once by O'Reilly. The England innings looked insecure
just now, and Ward was bowling his best this time, with
flight and spin. A half-hour or so of painful contention
happened while Barnett and Fagg kept guard against the
axe of O'Reilly and the skeleton key of Ward. Every ball,
we knew now, was a nail in somebody's coffin, England's
or Australia's. Fagg was gallantly dour and watchful, but
we could see Barnett chafing in the cordon of Australia's
counter attack. At last he made an attempt to escape. He hit

beautifully to leg, only to be caught deep and beautifully by Badcock. With a pretty off-drive, Fagg greeted Hammond. Dazzling fielding pounced on Hammond's shots. Here was a game fit for the gods at last, but charged with fatality.

---

### FOURTH DAY

#### ENGLAND First Innings

| | |
|---|---:|
| Worthington, c. Oldfield, b. McCormick | 0 |
| Barnett, c. Oldfield, b. O'Reilly | 69 |
| Fagg, c. Oldfield, b. McCormick | 4 |
| Hammond, c. Robinson, b. McCormick | 0 |
| Leyland, b. Ward | 126 |
| Ames, c. Chipperfield, b. Ward | 24 |
| Hardstaff, c. McCabe, b. O'Reilly | 43 |
| R. W. V. Robins, c. sub. (Brown), b. O'Reilly | 38 |
| G. O. Allen, c. McCabe, b. O'Reilly | 35 |
| Verity, c. Sievers, b. O'Reilly | 7 |
| Voce, not out | 4 |
| Extras (b. 1, l.b. 3, n.b. 4) | 8 |
| **Total** | **358** |

England first-innings bowling analysis

| | O. | M. | R. | W. |
|---|---:|---:|---:|---:|
| McCormick | 8 | 1 | 26 | 3 |
| Sievers | 16 | 5 | 42 | 0 |
| O'Reilly | 40·6 | 13 | 102 | 5 |
| Ward | 36 | 3 | 138 | 2 |
| Chipperfield | 11 | 3 | 32 | 0 |
| McCabe | 2 | 0 | 10 | 0 |

Fall of the wickets:

| 1 | 2 | 3 | 4 | 5 | 6 | 7 | 8 | 9 | 10 |
|---|---|---|---|---|---|---|---|---|---|
| 0 | 20 | 20 | 119 | 162 | 252 | 311 | 311 | 343 | 358 |

#### AUSTRALIA First Innings

| | |
|---|---:|
| J. H. Fingleton, b. Verity | 100 |
| C. L. Badcock, b. Allen | 8 |
| D. G. Bradman, c. Worthington, b. Voce | 38 |
| S. J. McCabe, c. Barnett, b. Voce | 51 |
| R. Robinson, c. Hammond, b. Voce | 2 |
| A. G. Chipperfield, c. Ames, b. Voce | 7 |

### AUSTRALIAN First Innings—*continued*

| | |
|---|---|
| M. Sievers, b. Allen . . . . . . | 8 |
| W. A. Oldfield, c. Ames, b. Voce . . . | 6 |
| W. J. O'Reilly, c. Leyland, b. Voce . . . | 3 |
| F. Ward, c. Hardstaff, b. Allen . . . . | 0 |
| E. L. McCormick, not out . . . . | 1 |
| Extras (b. 4, l.b. 1, n.b. 5) . . . . | 10 |
| **Total** . . . . . . | **234** |

#### Australia first-innings bowling analysis

| | O. | M. | R. | W. |
|---|---|---|---|---|
| Allen . . . | 16 | 2 | 71 | 3 |
| Voce . . . | 20·6 | 5 | 41 | 6 |
| Hammond . . | 4 | 0 | 12 | 0 |
| Verity . . . | 28 | 11 | 52 | 1 |
| Robins . . . | 17 | 0 | 48 | 0 |

#### Fall of the wickets:

| 1 | 2 | 3 | 4 | 5 | 6 | 7 | 8 | 9 | 10 |
|---|---|---|---|---|---|---|---|---|---|
| 13 | 89 | 166 | 176 | 202 | 220 | 229 | 231 | 231 | 234 |

### ENGLAND Second Innings

| | |
|---|---|
| Worthington, st. Oldfield, b. McCabe . . | 8 |
| Barnett, c. Badcock, b. Ward . . . . | 26 |
| Fagg, st. Oldfield, b. Ward . . . . | 27 |
| Hammond, hit wkt., b. Ward . . . . | 25 |
| Leyland, c. Bradman, b. Ward . . . . | 33 |
| Ames, b. Sievers . . . . . . | 9 |
| G. O. Allen, c. Fingleton, b. Sievers . . . | 68 |
| Hardstaff, st. Oldfield, b. Ward . . . . | 20 |
| R. W. V. Robins, c. Chipperfield, b. Ward . | 0 |
| Verity, l.b.w., b. Sievers . . . . | 19 |
| Voce, not out . . . . . . . | 2 |
| Extras (b. 14, l.b. 4, n.b. 1) . . . | 19 |
| **Total** . . . . . . | **256** |

#### England second-innings bowling analysis

| | O. | M. | R. | W. |
|---|---|---|---|---|
| Sievers . . . | 19·6 | 9 | 29 | 3 |
| McCabe . . | 6 | 1 | 14 | 1 |
| Ward . . . | 46 | 16 | 102 | 6 |
| O'Reilly . . | 35 | 15 | 59 | 0 |
| Chipperfield . . | 10 | 2 | 33 | 0 |

Fall of the wickets:

| 1 | 2 | 3 | 4 | 5 | 6 | 7 | 8 | 9 | 10 |
|---|---|---|---|---|---|---|---|---|-----|
| 17 | 50 | 82 | 105 | 122 | 144 | 205 | 205 | 247 | 256 |

AUSTRALIA SECOND INNINGS

| | | | | | | |
|---|---|---|---|---|---|---|
| J. H. Fingleton, b. Voce | . | . | . | . | . | 0 |
| C. L. Badcock, not out | . | . | . | . | . | 0 |
| M. Sievers, not out . | . | . | . | . | . | 2 |
| Extras . | . | . | . | . | . | 1 |

Total (for 1 wicket) . . . . 3

Fall of the wicket:

1
—
0

This day was a prolonged and variable argument. At first England seemed to have thrown away Monday's rich rewards. Magnificent bowling by Ward caused a return in the England batsmen of those pedal infirmities which reduced them to more or less immobile attitudes against slow spin at Sydney and Melbourne. The day was retrieved by Allen, whose innings, I think, was the best and bravest of his career.

Allen showed fight and, better still, footwork. His bat was not a suspicious shield, but a weapon of war. He played straight, and seldom, if ever, fell into the common error of groping for leg-breaks behind the crease. At the pinch, when England were still not far enough ahead in runs, Verity exerted a stern disapproving obstinacy, seeming to reprove the bowlers for their efforts to make an advance. Australia's attack began and ended with Ward, whose spin and flight, until he wearied, were as beautiful as no doubt they were devilish to counter.

When the match entered act four in the morning, the warmth was sticky as glucose, and Hammond at once drove

Chipperfield straight for four to the pavilion. But in Ward's first over, a lovely ball, perfectly pitched, drew Fagg forward. He didn't want to go forward; the curving temptation of the flight was beyond his powers of resistance. It was an immoral ball in its allurement, and Fagg was stumped by Oldfield, who is still the most stylish and most rapid wicket-keeper. If only Ward could bowl always as he bowled in this match! However, as Charles Fry says oracularly, much as Jack Bunsby says, 'notwithstanding'.

When Leyland became Hammond's companion, the match was poised precariously. A loss of one of these batsmen now would swing the game's balance Australia's way once more. The Australians bowled and fielded hard. O'Reilly, the windmill, laboured weightily upon the earth, and Ward not only twisted his fingers but also his face, in sympathetic accordance with the state of his mind. Only Oldfield put the bloom of artistic delight into the general antagonism; he flapped his gloves, walked his dapper straight-backed walk down the wicket between the overs, so like Charles Hawtrey in *Ambrose Applejohn*. And, speaking of wicket-keepers' gloves, I am reminded that the other day I was shown the gloves used by Blackham ages ago. They are not capacious and thick, like the modern contrivances. They are tiny, even delicate, the sort of gloves that Oldfield or Duckworth probably got married in.

The atmosphere of England's innings thickened stuffily. I felt too much the presence of the policy of 'what we have we'll hold'. O'Reilly gnawed at Leyland's leg-stump, with four fieldsmen forming an accessory square. At a quarter to one, Ward's length and spin forced Hammond on to the stumps: Hammond stabbed late at the ball in his own back-footed, short-armed way, and he hit the stumps. The bowler deserved his luck. As Hammond left the crease his face was a tablet of unutterable thoughts. England had lost their advantage. I was afraid on Monday that they would allow the idea of making assurance doubly sure to run to the passive length that encourages the opposition and makes counter-attacks not difficult for canny bowlers. The Adelaide match, and the rubber, was lost this way. I felt a negative plan at work: the only consolation was the sign in Ward's bowling that the wicket did not always ignore spin. But the amount of back-play and pad-play recalled England's worst experience a week or two earlier, against Mudge and Fudge and the rest.

During lunch, the impression was advertised that the England batsmen were not blaming the wicket for their troubles. They praised Ward, which was very nice of them. But good bowling must be expected, as a matter of course, in any Test match, especially when Australia are fighting to regain a lost position. After the interval, Leyland strove at once to put new spirit into the situation. In the morning he had batted eighty minutes for 19. Now he lifted up his bat and assumed an attitude of belligerency. Alas, it was not a favourable day for him. He jumped into Ward, hit high to the on, where Bradman ran across and into the ball, catching it gloriously, throwing it up as if the game were already won. It was good to see Bradman for a moment in the outfield, away from the confined places of the wicket which are the captain's house of legislature. In England we loved his little frog crouch on the boundary between the fall of wickets, and his speed in the chase and his returns.

Hardstaff did not begin easy of mind against Ward, and when Ward needed a rest after twenty consecutive and artistic overs, Hardstaff scarcely liked Chipperfield any better. All the while Allen struggled like a leader, gallantly brave. Moreover, he had the sense to play forward at least as frequently as he played back. Again the strain of the match increased; some patron saint aloft was holding up his arms for one side or the other to bring victory by the sign. But for which side was he watching and praying? Every ball was vital now, and Australia gave nothing away. The match had been a pretty see-saw; England three for 20 on Friday, then the retaliation, then Australia's breakdown, and now—what?

While Chipperfield and Sievers bowled, and O'Reilly and Ward refreshed their loins, Hardstaff came out of a fifty minutes' dream and showed us some lovely strokes. When O'Reilly attacked again, Allen hit him square for four, a magnificent blow, and a captain's. Allen's cricket was an example to those of his team who had fallen through too much circumspection and back-play. He used his feet and his eye; he was courageous and imaginative. He inspired Hardstaff, who waited for Ward and cut him fiercely. Here, surely, was the game at the great turning point, the sea at the secret turn of the tide.

Hardstaff was suddenly stumped reaching out from a rigid foothold to Ward. Now Verity came in with his hair sticking up at the back of his head, like the hero of my boyhood, Reggie Spooner. England were 339 ahead, and it was necessary for Australia to wind up and settle at once. But Verity ignored all invitations to get out. He played with academic mien, and if now and then he edged a ball, it was only a case of his mortar-board getting a little awry under stress of the moment's cerebration. He did his side service, and Allen went his heroic course, a leader with a hearty disbelief in giving things up.

He went to his end after Verity absent-mindedly forgot to stay in. He banged for death or glory, and was caught with a flourish, a right and proper end for an innings plucky and strong.

At the day's end, in a fading light with clouds on high, Australia set about her long task, and sad and shocking was the beginning. The hero of the first innings, Jack Fingleton, was bowled first ball by Voce. He was much too late. Then there were subtle consultations about the light between the umpires; they might have been metaphysicians discussing the phenomenal universe. They decided that the weather was dark and so the fourth day ended.

---

## FIFTH DAY

### ENGLAND First Innings

| | |
|---|---|
| Worthington, c. Oldfield, b. McCormick | 0 |
| Barnett, c. Oldfield, b. O'Reilly | 69 |
| Fagg, c. Oldfield, b. McCormick | 4 |
| Hammond, c. Robinson, b. McCormick | 0 |
| Leyland, b. Ward | 126 |
| Ames, c. Chipperfield, b. Ward | 24 |
| Hardstaff, c. McCabe, b. O'Reilly | 43 |
| R. W. V. Robins, c. sub. (Brown), b. O'Reilly | 38 |
| G. O. Allen, c. McCabe, b. O'Reilly | 35 |
| Verity, c. Sievers, b. O'Reilly | 7 |
| Voce, not out | 4 |
| Extras (b. 1, l.b. 3, n.b. 4) | 8 |
| Total | 358 |

England first-innings bowling analysis

| | O. | M. | R. | W. |
|---|---|---|---|---|
| McCormick | 8 | 1 | 26 | 3 |
| Sievers | 16 | 5 | 42 | 0 |
| O'Reilly | 40.6 | 13 | 102 | 5 |
| Ward | 36 | 3 | 138 | 2 |
| Chipperfield | 11 | 3 | 32 | 0 |
| McCabe | 2 | 0 | 10 | 0 |

Fall of the wickets:

| 1 | 2 | 3 | 4 | 5 | 6 | 7 | 8 | 9 | 10 |
|---|---|---|---|---|---|---|---|---|---|
| 0 | 20 | 20 | 119 | 162 | 252 | 311 | 311 | 343 | 358 |

## AUSTRALIA First Innings

| | |
|---|---:|
| J. H. Fingleton, b. Verity . . . . . | 100 |
| C. L. Badcock, b. Allen . . . . . | 8 |
| D. G. Bradman, c. Worthington, b. Voce . . | 38 |
| S. J. McCabe, c. Barnett, b. Voce . . . | 51 |
| R. Robinson, c. Hammond, b. Voce . . . | 2 |
| A. G. Chipperfield, c. Ames, b. Voce . . . | 7 |
| M. Sievers, b. Allen . . . . . . | 8 |
| W. A. Oldfield, c. Ames, b. Voce . . . | 6 |
| W. J. O'Reilly, c. Leyland, b. Voce . . . | 3 |
| F. Ward, c. Hardstaff, b. Allen . . . . | 0 |
| E. L. McCormick, not out . . . . | 1 |
| Extras (b. 4, l.b. 1, n.b. 5) . . . . | 10 |
| Total . . . . . . | 234 |

### Australia first-innings bowling analysis

| | O. | M. | R. | W. |
|---|---|---|---|---|
| Allen . . . | 16 | 2 | 71 | 3 |
| Voce . . . | 20·6 | 5 | 41 | 6 |
| Hammond . . | 4 | 0 | 12 | 0 |
| Verity . . . | 28 | 11 | 52 | 1 |
| Robins . . . | 17 | 0 | 48 | 0 |

### Fall of the wickets:

| 1 | 2 | 3 | 4 | 5 | 6 | 7 | 8 | 9 | 10 |
|---|---|---|---|---|---|---|---|---|---|
| 13 | 89 | 166 | 176 | 202 | 220 | 229 | 231 | 231 | 234 |

## ENGLAND Second Innings

| | |
|---|---:|
| Worthington, st. Oldfield, b. McCabe . . | 8 |
| Barnett, c. Badcock, b. Ward . . . | 26 |
| Fagg, st. Oldfield, b. Ward . . . | 27 |
| Hammond, hit wkt., b. Ward . . . | 25 |
| Leyland, c. Bradman, b. Ward . . . | 33 |
| Ames, b. Sievers . . . . . | 9 |
| G. O. Allen, c. Fingleton, b. Sievers . . | 68 |
| Hardstaff, st. Oldfield, b. Ward . . . | 20 |
| R. W. V. Robins, c. Chipperfield, b. Ward . | 0 |
| Verity, l.b.w., b. Sievers . . . . | 19 |
| Voce, not out . . . . . . | 2 |
| Extras (b. 14, l.b. 4, n.b. 1) . . . | 19 |
| Total . . . . . . | 256 |

England second-innings bowling analysis

|  | O. | M. | R. | W. |
|---|---|---|---|---|
| Sievers . . . | 19·6 | 9 | 29 | 3 |
| McCabe . . | 6 | 1 | 14 | 1 |
| Ward . . . | 46 | 16 | 102 | 6 |
| O'Reilly . . | 35 | 15 | 59 | 0 |
| Chipperfield . . | 10 | 2 | 33 | 0 |

Fall of the wickets:

| 1 | 2 | 3 | 4 | 5 | 6 | 7 | 8 | 9 | 10 |
|---|---|---|---|---|---|---|---|---|---|
| 17 | 50 | 82 | 105 | 122 | 144 | 205 | 205 | 247 | 256 |

### AUSTRALIA Second Innings

| | |
|---|---|
| J. H. Fingleton, b. Voce . . . . . | 0 |
| C. L. Badcock, c. Fagg, b. Allen . . . | 0 |
| M. Sievers, c. Voce, b. Allen . . . . | 5 |
| W. A. Oldfield, b. Voce . . . . . | 10 |
| D. G. Bradman, c. Fagg, b. Allen . . | 0 |
| S. J. McCabe, c. Leyland, b. Allen . . . | 7 |
| R. Robinson, c. Hammond, b. Voce . . . | 3 |
| A. G. Chipperfield, not out . . . | 26 |
| F. Ward, b. Voce . . . . . . | 1 |
| E. L. McCormick, absent hurt . . . . | 0 |
| W. J. O'Reilly, b. Allen . . . . . | 0 |
| Extras (n.b. 6) . . . . . | 6 |
| Total . . . . . . | 58 |

Australia second-innings bowling analysis

|  | O. | M. | R. | W. |
|---|---|---|---|---|
| Allen . . . | 6 | 0 | 36 | 5 |
| Voce . . . | 6·3 | 0 | 16 | 4 |

Fall of the wickets:

| 1 | 2 | 3 | 4 | 5 | 6 | 7 | 8 | 9 | — |
|---|---|---|---|---|---|---|---|---|---|
| 0 | 3 | 7 | 7 | 16 | 20 | 35 | 41 | 58 | 58 |

England won easily, thanks in part to the advent of rain, which caused the ball to rear geometrically. I am sorry the weather broke. After the uphill fight from the terrible prelude, England deserved a chance to force home an undoubted advantage in circumstances which did not leave

victory in any way open to detraction. Allen and Voce
made the most of their opportunity and easy prey.

At the beginning of the day, the wicket was softer than
many experts had expected it to be. Allen's first ball
jumped, and the second skidded to the base of Badcock's
bat, and sped thence by percussive law to the exultant grip
of Fagg in the slips. To the general surprise, Bradman did
not come in next. Perhaps he wished to save his assets until
the turf lost whatever venom it may have possessed. To the
slaughter came Oldfield, upright and philosophical. Voce
bowled at Allen's opposite end, the idea, no doubt, being to
knock pieces out of the pitch in readiness for Verity. But
there was a prospect that Verity would not be needed:
in Allen's second over Sievers put his bat without rational
intent to an ordinary good length outswinger which made
haste from the ground. And now came Bradman himself—
and succumbed to his second ball, also from Allen. It
kicked to the region of his bat's shoulder, and he could do
nothing but stab instinctively, as purposeless as a man
flicking at the gyrations of a wasp or mosquito. He was
caught joyfully by Fagg, and Allen hugged himself.

Australia were 7 for four: arbitrary interference from the
outside was spoiling four days of good fighting, in conditions which had showed no partisan favour. When the
total or aggregate was 16 McCabe tried to pull to leg a
ball from Allen, which reared after pitching short to leg.
His stroke was hurried and bad and not over his object.

No doubt the wicket made impossible the authentic
easeful stroke-play of Australia. None the less, the batting
was grotesquely at a loss to deal with the occasion's
difficulties. Robinson even endeavoured to hook a ball
while it was rising acutely towards his breastbone. Once on
a time Australian batsmen were known to come to England

in a season of sticky wickets and win a rubber against the finest bowlers we have ever boasted. In 1902 Victor Trumper cut and drove century after century on terrible English fields in spite of Lockwood, Blythe, Rhodes, Walter Mead, and the rest.

There was sense and courage in Chipperfield's cricket. He drove Allen to the off in strong style, then skied him high as a tower over the slips, a frustrated on-drive. It was Chipperfield who gave aid to Woodfull at Lord's in 1934, on a day which saw Australia helpless on a Verity wicket. Ward was struck in the face from an abrupt 'kicker' from Allen, which was not only a misfortune to him but one also to Allen, for so far his and Voce's attack had seldom, if ever, endangered the general physiognomy. The pitch was nasty rather than brutish.

At one o'clock the match was over. The morning suggested certain ironies. What did poor Verity think about it all? Allen did not intend to bowl unchanged. He went on to help get the shine off the ball for Verity. When he took the wickets of Sievers, Badcock, and Bradman in two overs, he could not believe the evidence of his senses. Verity, who spent Sunday in Brisbane praying for rain (with the parsons and the inhabitants), never got a chance.

## CHAPTER IX

# SECOND TEST—SYDNEY

### *December 18–22, 1936*

---

### *FIRST DAY*

#### ENGLAND First Innings

| | |
|---|---|
| Fagg, c. Sievers, b. McCormick . . . . | 11 |
| Barnett, b. Ward . . . . . . | 57 |
| Hammond, not out . . . . . . | 167 |
| Leyland, l.b.w. (n.), b. McCabe . . . | 42 |
| Ames, not out . . . . . . . | 14 |
| Extras . . . . . . . | 16 |
| Total (for 3 wickets) . . . . | 307 |

To bat.—G. O. Allen, R. W. V. Robins, Hardstaff, Sims, Verity, and Voce.

Fall of the wickets:

| 1 | 2 | 3 |
|---|---|---|
| 27 | 118 | 247 |

ENGLAND again won the toss, and the wicket was the brownest, the most arid, I have known; a blade of grass on it would have appeared an oasis, a refreshing mirage seen in a sentimental Englishman's delirium. In fact, at first I thought the wicket had been brought in a packing-case from the middle of the desert which divides Perth from Adelaide.

McCormick again made the ball bounce upwards. He caressed the lobe of Fagg's left ear; also, he swung so far to leg that Oldfield elongated his body to save the byes. Barnett pushed Sievers elegantly for four to the off, a persuasive rather than a propulsive hit; then Fagg leaned forward to McCormick and scored three also in front of the wicket. No fast bowler on this resilient earth should have allowed such a liberty.

McCormick bowled with so much persistence to leg that when at half-past twelve he compelled a ball to run away to the off, my surprise was probably equal to that of Fagg, who edged fatally to the slips. The crowd promptly roared Fagg out of sight, and roared Hammond into full and expectant public view. Barnett greeted him with a great hit off McCormick, a drive past the covers from the back foot, a Hammond stroke, as though the red corpuscles in it had been acquired and assimilated by Barnett through some miracle of blood transfusion.

The crowd rejoiced in a spacious sweep to leg off Ward. It was good to be at Sydney for a Test match, with the field the focal point of a multitude's interest, desires, and aspirations; the December sky an immensity of blue; the 'Hill' gathering its strength; and the little flower-beds in front of the pavilion like so many cautiously detached emblems of domestic peace in a raging universe of sport.

Ward beat Barnett with a spinner to the off, and one or two slashes by Barnett lent to his cricket a momentary sense of aberration. O'Reilly wheeled himself into action just before one o'clock, and drinks were conveyed into the sultry middle. And here I suddenly had a vision of England, away at the earth's other end, deep in the winter's night. Often in other years I have lain in bed in the enfeebled breathing of two o'clock in the December morning, and beheld a vision of Sydney and cricket and sunshine, far distant, under the world.

O'Reilly wrinkled the brow of Hammond's innings, and Chipperfield made a heroic effort to catch Barnett from a mishit off a leg-spinner high in the air, over first and only slip. I was not altogether easy in mind about England's batting hereabout. A lovely variation by O'Reilly, so artfully floated and disguised in pace that it seemed to travel by syncopations, drew Hammond forward, and his bat played too soon, sending a half-chance to Fingleton at silly short leg. Fingleton flattened and stretched himself on a rack of endeavour, but he could only touch the ball. Hammond was not happy, not doing the things he wanted to do, and Barnett's innings became a fascinating study in light and shade, free shots and crabbed shots, some in the middle of the bat and one on the oil-hole. But Barnett's good strokes were glorious. His range is wider than Hammond's, and always he is a batsman who prefers to enjoy, rather than suffer, his cricket.

McCormick returned to the fray at 89, and at once a long-hop sped upwards to Barnett. The crowd emitted curious piercing noises as the ball bounced aimlessly near the slips. I do not think that McCormick made the most of his opportunities before lunch. He should surely have aimed at or just outside the off stump, and raised the hopes of his slips instead of hurling long-hops to leg, where sometimes all of Oldfield's agility was needed to reach them. After the interval, McCormick's pace dwindled. His bowling became laboured and middle-aged. He created the illusion of a quieter and reformed wicket. At half-past two, the crowd was a noble spectacle seen from the lofty eminence of the Press box, where we dwelt like hot-house growths under glass, our adjectives a mass of colour, because of labour and heat.

A sonorous roar announced the downfall of Barnett. Ward dispatched him with a googly. Barnett's innings had beauty and chivalry in it, but he still needs to smooth out his technique and achieve a nice correspondence between conception and execution. He is periodically inclined to hit at the ball when it is a little distant from him. None the less, here is one of the handsomest English batsmen seen on an Australian cricket field since A. C. MacLaren was lord of all, dismissing the fast rising attack of Ernest Jones from his presence.

Hammond could not for a long time assert his mastery. His strokes were not born as though by unburdened creative means. This was hard, responsible work, governed by thought and experience, not by instinct. It was like a poet's official ode for an occasion. When he was in the forties, Hammond tried to drive Ward to the off. The stroke was carried by spin perilously beyond slip. There was material weight in Hammond's bat, and material anxiety. 'Why can we not soar?' asked Mr. Chadband, and Mr. Jellyby helpfully suggested, 'No wings'. Hammond's cricket to-day walked the encompassed earth.

O'Reilly aimed at his leg stump persistently, but not with the guile he was to show later in the tour. The Australian bowling appeared to be generally short of constructive ideas. Leyland again was canny; every one of his defensive products and pushes said, in Yorkshire, 'Nay, lad, ah'm having none'. With the passing of Barnett, the lancers and cavalry departed for a while. The warfare went into the trenches, behind the sandbags, and O'Reilly sweated away like a tired but dutiful sergeant-major. I could discern no spin in his work, only a patient hope for something to happen on, or in the vicinity of, the leg stump.

Hammond's century, which arrived in the course of time, was not one of his consummate performances. But it stirred admiration because it had to be built up by concentrated effort. The masterpieces of genius are easy. We revel in them, but render them no honour by relating them to deeds done at the expense of mortal and fallible toil. Hammond to-day was a man attending to a job of work. Perhaps he was bored by it all; that is, if these cricketers are aware that they become on occasions artists and liberators of the spirit. There was almost a moral excellence about Hammond's determination this afternoon to stay in and do service to his captain and colleagues.

The new ball was available after tea, and McCormick proceeded to waste it by bowling so wide that the batsmen could only have got into danger by feats acrobatic and harmful to the delicate organization of the human anatomy. But Hammond made one remarkable stroke off McCormick. He chopped late on a widish off-side half-volley, and with bent knees achieved a rasping four past point. It was a Tower Hill stroke. You could almost see the axe and the block.

## SECOND DAY

### ENGLAND FIRST INNINGS

| | |
|---|---:|
| Fagg, c. Sievers, b. McCormick . . . . | 11 |
| Barnett, b. Ward . . . . . . | 57 |
| Hammond, not out . . . . . . | 231 |
| Leyland, l.b.w. (b.), b. McCabe . . . . | 42 |
| Ames, c. sub., b. Ward . . . . . | 29 |
| G. O. Allen, l.b.w., b. O'Reilly . . . . | 9 |
| Hardstaff, b. McCormick . . . . . | 26 |
| Verity, not out. . . . . . . | 0 |
| Extras (b. 8, l.b. 8, n.b. 4, w. 1) . . . | 21 |
| | |
| Total (for 6 wickets) . . . . | 426 |

To bat.—R. W. V. Robins, Voce, Sims.

England first-innings bowling analysis to date

| | O. | M. | R. | W. |
|---|---:|---:|---:|---:|
| McCormick . . | 20 | 1 | 79 | 2 |
| Sievers . . . | 16·2 | 4 | 30 | 0 |
| Ward . . . | 42 | 8 | 132 | 2 |
| O'Reilly . . | 41 | 17 | 86 | 1 |
| Chipperfield . . | 13 | 2 | 47 | 0 |
| McCabe . . | 9 | 1 | 31 | 1 |

Fall of the wickets:

| 1 | 2 | 3 | 4 | 5 | 6 |
|---|---|---|---|---|---|
| 27 | 118 | 247 | 351 | 368 | 424 |

Sometimes, especially when England are batting, the governing idea in an Australian Test match seems to be that if you win the toss and go in first, runs are a secondary matter; the main consideration is to stay at the crease for hours and hours, and wear out the wicket, not until it merely develops spots, but until it cracks and so subsides that a seismographic instrument in Peking will register a severe disturbance of the earth's crust at Sydney.

To-day the game had for a while a stilted solemnity; the field was set deep for conjectural boundaries; and near the batsmen's right trouser pockets two fieldsmen crouched in the leg trap, intense and almost breaking blood-vessels with expectancy. They seldom got a ghost of a catch, but they remained intense. Nobody smiled; indeed, if anybody had smiled I should have expected one of the umpires to clear the ground, adding, 'This place is not a theatre'.

McCormick toiled hard, but his pace was somehow checked, and he could not make the ball rise; he seemed weary and uncertain of shoulder and limb. O'Reilly came to his relief at half-past twelve. On the first day, he had seemed to be training for the post of Australia's fast bowler; this time his flight described an ampler curve, and again he aimed at the leg stump. Much more artistic was the spin of Ward; he nearly got Hammond caught by Chipperfield at slip; there was a great roar, which was a compliment to Hammond; but the ball dropped safely in front of Fingleton, the fieldsman, who, quick as a monkey, tried to run Hammond out. A stately girl near me said: 'Bloody smart work'.

A strong and beautiful point of Hammond's innings was his sweeps to leg; he pulled O'Reilly round with a sumptuous rhythm, and then, as a variation, hit him past point; here was the true Hammond, as handsome as a cricketer well could be, with the classic poise, calm and impersonal austerity. The reserve power of his drives was impressive; he played forward to spin on the lightest feet, head over the danger point, and his bat was straight and apparently alive with feelers—cat's whiskers, delicate organs of sensibility.

Though the Australian fielding was individually good, the returns often lacked direction; fortunately Oldfield was at his best, whether behind the wicket, or at mid-on, or deep square leg. McCabe bowled instead of Ward, and occasionally he experimented privately with a leg-break; one of them turned quickly to Ames and jumped a little, whereat Ames walked out of his ground and examined the pitch. Batsmen nowadays should be supplied by the umpire with magnifying lenses and spirit levels.

During the warm morning's first hour, England scored 47, Hammond 35, Ames 10. In spite of Hammond's style, the Test match unities were being respected. Hammond made his aggregate 2000 in Test matches against Australia, at least I was told as much: my first impression was that he was making them all now.

A marvellous throw-in by Bradman was one of the flashing deeds of the occasion; then, next ball, Ames slashed a poor leg-spinner from Ward straight to cover; the ball was on the short side, and asked for chastisement. Ames's stroke was careless, and when he saw his end he cursed himself with an eloquent bat; the morning's work had been slightly spoiled. Just after half-past two, O'Reilly acquired a wicket. He got Allen l.b.w. when Allen had played forward and somehow missed his aim; the ball was well up. The occurrence seemed to take years from O'Reilly's shoulders. He plunged to the crease next ball like a man fresh from Dr. Steinach, and the women in the crowd shrieked terribly when Fingleton caught Hardstaff from a bump ball. As many women may be seen at a Test match in Australia as in Oxford Street during the January sales.

The Australian attack improved; there was room for it. Before lunch it had seemed inaccurate and rather bankrupt of ideas. Once or twice the right length was achieved, and then I thought the wicket was already taking spin. And all the time, over after over, Hammond went his serene way; I cannot remember batsmanship of surer and more easeful technique than Hammond's this day. There was no strain, even though he was carrying the team; no haste and no lagging; every stroke and every movement of the feet and arms were now the instinctive expressions of a mastery which worked almost like a force in nature, needing to labour as little as the sunshine overhead, for the full light it shed on the England innings. At three o'clock a heavy shower of rain swept the players from sight; where it came from I could not say; in England we are given due notice of rain. I had not so far taken serious notice of cloud effects in Australia; my view of them is that they come into the sky solely to help Australian landscape artists with their light and shade. And, by the way, Australia has many fine landscape painters.

The game was interrupted only ten minutes, and when the match proceeded there was momentarily no sunshine, a curious event in a cricket match in Australia; it was like watching a play with the footlights turned out. At once the ball began to jump a little, and Hammond twice had to exercise his shrewdest skill against O'Reilly, and a close field was set. The slightly changed conditions obviously troubled the batsmen; Hardstaff was badly missed from a pull off O'Reilly to Robinson at square leg; the score was 394 for five, and Hardstaff 11. Then Hammond, when he was 205, sent a low and declined return to Ward, and in the same over a severe straight drive was not accepted by the umpire.

Hammond's chance, by the way, was his first serious error, and it needed the miracle of rain to bring it about. Hardstaff was again hesitant, and apparently unable to play a really hard stroke. The ball turned queerly hereabout and popped, but Hardstaff had not been altogether convincing before the showers. The wholly defensive methods of Hammond and Hardstaff at this moment stimulated the 'Hill', who at last found voice. After tea McCormick took the new ball and shot Hardstaff's off stump yards out of the ground; in the same over Verity edged a glorious outswinger, and, wonderful to relate, Oldfield missed a chance. The next ball reared diagonally at Hammond's breastbone, and Hammond stabbed it down with a bat which surely emitted a round oath. This was a fiery over, hostile as a battle-axe. The rain was falling heavily; in England we should all have run promptly; the players stood it like amphibians for five minutes, then they fled unanimously. That was the end of the afternoon; but the sun was shining when I left the ground and walked down an avenue of palm trees outside and caught a taxi and drove to Usher's.

## THIRD DAY

### ENGLAND First Innings

| | |
|---|---:|
| Fagg, c. Sievers, b. McCormick . . . . | 11 |
| Barnett, b. Ward . . . . . | 57 |
| Hammond, not out . . . . . | 231 |
| Leyland, l.b.w. (n.), b. McCabe . . . | 42 |
| Ames, c. sub., b. Ward . . . . | 29 |
| G. O. Allen, l.b.w., b. O'Reilly . . . | 9 |
| Hardstaff, b. McCormick . . . . | 26 |
| Verity, not out. . . . . . | 0 |
| Extras (b. 8, l.b. 8, n.b. 4, w. 1) . . . | 21 |

Total (for 6 wickets) . . . . 426

Innings declared closed.

Did not bat.—R. W. V. Robins, Voce, Sims.

England first-innings bowling analysis

| | O. | M. | R. | W. |
|---|---|---|---|---|
| McCormick . . | 20 | 1 | 79 | 2 |
| Sievers . . . | 16·2 | 4 | 30 | 0 |
| Ward . . . | 42 | 8 | 132 | 2 |
| O'Reilly . . | 41 | 17 | 86 | 1 |
| Chipperfield . . | 13 | 2 | 47 | 0 |
| McCabe . . | 9 | 1 | 31 | 1 |

Fall of the wickets:

| 1 | 2 | 3 | 4 | 5 | 6 |
|---|---|---|---|---|---|
| 27 | 118 | 247 | 351 | 368 | 424 |

### AUSTRALIA First Innings

| | |
|---|---:|
| J. H. Fingleton, c. Verity, b. Voce . . . | 12 |
| L. P. O'Brien, c. Sims, b. Voce . . . | 0 |
| D. G. Bradman, c. Allen, b. Voce . . . | 0 |
| S. J. McCabe, c. Sims, b. Voce . . . | 0 |
| A. G. Chipperfield, c. Sims, b. Allen . . | 13 |
| M. Sievers, c. Voce, b. Verity . . . | 4 |
| W. A. Oldfield, b. Verity . . . . | 1 |
| W. J. O'Reilly, not out . . . . | 37 |
| E. L. McCormick, b. Allen . . . | 10 |
| F. Ward, b. Allen . . . . | 0 |
| C. L. Badcock, absent ill . . . . | 0 |
| Extras (b. 1, l.b. 1, n.b. 1) . . . | 3 |

Total . . . . . 80

Australia first-innings bowling analysis

|         | O. | M. | R. | W. |
|---------|----|----|----|----|
| Voce . . . | 8 | 1 | 10 | 4 |
| Allen . . . | 5·7 | 1 | 19 | 3 |
| Verity . . . | 3 | 0 | 17 | 2 |
| Hammond . . | 4 | 0 | 6 | 0 |
| Sims . . . | 2 | 0 | 20 | 0 |
| Robins . . . | 1 | 0 | 5 | 0 |

Fall of the wickets:

| 1 | 2 | 3 | 4 | 5 | 6 | 7 | 8 | 9 |
|---|---|---|---|---|---|---|---|---|
| 1 | 1 | 1 | 16 | 28 | 30 | 31 | 80 | 80 |

## AUSTRALIA Second Innings

| J. H. Fingleton, not out . . . . . | 67 |
|---|---|
| L. P. O'Brien, c. Allen, b. Hammond . . | 17 |
| D. G. Bradman, not out . . . . . | 57 |
| Extras . . . . . . . | 4 |
| Total (for 1 wicket) . . . . | 145 |

To bat.—S. J. McCabe, A. G. Chipperfield, M. Sievers, W. A. Oldfield, W. J. O'Reilly, E. L. McCormick, F. Ward, C. L. Badcock.

Australia second-innings bowling analysis to date

|         | O. | M. | R. | W. |
|---------|----|----|----|----|
| Voce . . . | 7 | 2 | 15 | 0 |
| Allen . . . | 11 | 2 | 34 | 0 |
| Hammond . . | 4 | 0 | 10 | 1 |
| Sims . . . | 5 | 0 | 35 | 0 |
| Verity . . . | 12 | 3 | 38 | 0 |
| Robins . . . | 1 | 0 | 9 | 0 |

Fall of the wickets:

| 1 |
|---|
| 38 |

In the early hours of the morning I was awakened by the sound of music, the sweetest I had heard since I left England and Sir Thomas Beecham, airs and harmonies as grateful to the ear as Handel's 'Water Music'. Australian rain, torrents of summer, as the poet says. At first the sportsman in me argued with the patriot: 'It is not fair that Australia should again be trapped on anything like a bowler's pitch'. But then the patriot and the sportsman in me agreed that the Australian batsmen sorely needed practice on a moist wicket, and here was a Heaven-sent opportunity for them.

Allen of course declared his innings closed, and at noon, in moist feverish weather, the agony was resumed, and Voce with his seventh ball got O'Brien caught in the slips from a not at all devastating outswinger. O'Brien merely hung out his bat, hoping for the best. Voce's eighth ball was eminently respectable; it merely came upwards towards Bradman's left hip. No doubt it hung a little, but it was as harmless a ball as ever scuttled a great player. Bradman made an amiable Christmas present to Allen at short leg. I was not pleased by this occurrence. I have admired Bradman's cricket for years, and have invoked the muses to aid me in my efforts at truthful, if empurpled, praise. But Bradman's stroke was not fit for public view. It spoke of little hope, little resource.

In Voce's second over, McCabe perished to a most spasmodic thrust at an ordinary off-side ball, which would have been left alone by any cricketer possessed of his senses. Not one of these disasters to Australia could be related to the state of the wicket—only to the state of the minds of the batsmen. It was a relief when Chipperfield drove Allen boldly for four to the off. Nobody wished to see to-day another general hauling down of the Australian colours before Verity could come into action. A brilliant cut by Chipperfield from Voce was like a gallant retaliatory broadside from the battered ship. He deserved his luck when Fagg badly missed him in the same over at second slip. But Chipperfield could not make capital of his fortune. He fell to an off-side catch from an entirely irrational stab or flick. This cricket made me ill to see. I was brought up on Trumper, Duff, Darling, and only yesterday I saw Macartney and Bardsley.

When Australia was 16 for four, at half-past twelve, the evidence we had witnessed of a really difficult wicket could have been written on a postage stamp. The collapse was the more reprehensible because Allen was far below his true form: he over-tossed and could only now and again hasten a stroke. Indeed, I received the impression from Allen's attack that the wicket was as well behaved as a censored Australian novel. Fingleton played the lonely game, which up to now was almost a stock part for him. His cool treatment of an over of Voce at a quarter to one convinced me that the wicket had been libelled. Only the complete long-hop rose with any obtuseness of angle.

Verity bowled at 23, and Fingleton drove a half-volley straight for four. Not a single ball of the eight obeyed the blandishments of Verity's fingers. Fingleton succumbed to a good ball from Voce, an outswinger which he tried to drive. It veered away late, and perhaps Fingleton did not go far enough across. A pitiful hour's batting, worse even than the Brisbane stampede.

Sievers was caught on the off-side from a number eleven hit of ripe vintage: the ball was about the first which Verity turned. And Oldfield was out cleaving across a potential full toss with a cross-bat, which brought to my mind visions of rustic England, the old tithe barn, the spreading chestnut tree, and the village blacksmith.

O'Reilly came in, and at once smote a huge six from Verity, whose spinless bowling was proof that the wicket was, at any rate, no use to him. The worst that could be said of it was that it enabled Voce to lift the ball from time to time, not alarmingly, but for the most part at an angle announced by the length. Verity was actually taken off while O'Reilly and McCormick were batting; an eloquent sign for us. The sun was behind the cloud now. Another storm seemed brewing. Voce rested after seventy-five minutes' work, with the grand and ridiculous analysis of 8 overs, 1 maiden, 10 runs, 4 wickets. The match now degenerated into a slogging bout. Sims came on and Hardstaff missed McCormick off him—a difficult running catch at the obscure position of deep mid-wicket. O'Reilly clouted the next ball for six: the crowd roared, and, of course, these hefty methods were better than nothing, even though it changed Sydney temporarily into a fair-ground, and planted cricket's head through the yokel's horse-collar. Allen, I think, made a mistake by letting Sims bowl at a left-handed smiter. Had he himself gone on when Voce tired, we might have had the lowest Australian score in an Australian Test match.

During the lunch interval several judges of the game, in a position to give an opinion of authority, described the wicket as slowish and easy of pace. That was rather an exaggeration. Voce, with the new ball, obtained a lively rise, but not one which was out of the common. And frankly, the bowling at the other end was poor, until Hammond got more life out of the earth than anybody else. After lunch, Allen peculiarly called on Robins, and more runs were given away. Test match cricket of more suspicious quality could not well be imagined. A few minutes after half-past two, the end came to one of the most inglorious pages in Australian cricket history. Badcock could not bat, and O'Reilly enjoyed three sixes, and somehow his innings gave us the proper ironical commentary on what we had, with abashed eyes, seen.

The wicket rolled out nicely for Australia's second innings. I had almost expected England to go in again, and Allen took a dangerous and unnecessary risk. Fingleton and O'Brien batted quietly, suggesting a cooler view of things. But Fagg missed O'Brien in the slips, and Fingleton performed a primitive heave at an off-drive ball. He must make a present of the stroke to O'Reilly. It might become quite good when left-handed. Allen was not impressive. I felt now a great chance was at hand for an Australian rally and recovery, especially when an over by Sims was plundered to the sum of 15. The crowd roared hoarsely and lost voice altogether when Hammond came on and got O'Brien caught at short square leg. Hammond's bowling was as good as any of the day. He made Bradman hurry himself to play the first ball, a fine break-back. Bradman was guilty also of a perilous push through the slips off Hammond when only six. But Allen trusts to speed at the beginning of a Bradman innings, and Voce was called back. As a fact, Hammond got a greater vitality than Voce from the pitch.

Though Allen himself joined in the barrage again, the wicket could not have been sweeter-tempered now, and the English attack appeared a little circumscribed. It was bound to get into trouble sooner or later. Allen should certainly have batted again. After tea, Bradman made a stroke of genius from Allen. He jumped across the stumps and hit an off-side ball in front of square leg with the timing of the tiger. Then Fingleton drove Allen straight for a gallant four; he is a brave, patient batsman, who never plays to the gallery, and is ready to do his bit in fair or foul weather. I have little regard for those cricketers who wait for the favourable hour and for the perfect wicket. Fingleton is the kind of man I should want in my side when the odds were against us. The bowler has to get him out. He does not bend to the unfriendly wind. He is growing out of the off-side flick that has so often betrayed him in the past.

Bradman delighted us with several personal strokes without convincing us that he was yet entirely himself. He batted eighty minutes for 34, and committed a stroke through the slips off Verity which for all he knew was the end of him. The difference between Don to-day and the Don of six years ago is that occasionally you can see how the great man might somehow be got out.

Fingleton reached an honourable 50, amid applause, and celebrated it with a lovely off-drive. A minute later a beautiful spinner from Verity missed Bradman's off stump by an inch. That night, wise men in Sydney maintained that Australia after all would win; that Allen had committed the gravest blunder by allowing Australia to follow on, with the wicket improved to harmlessness. The wise men told one another this argument many times, as though anxious to convince themselves as well as us.

---

## FOURTH DAY

### ENGLAND First Innings

| | | | | |
|---|---|---|---|---|
| Fagg, c. Sievers, b. McCormick . | . | . | . | 11 |
| Barnett, b. Ward . | . | . | . | 57 |
| Hammond, not out . | . | . | . | 231 |
| Leyland, l.b.w. (n.), b. McCabe . | . | . | . | 42 |
| Ames, c. sub., b. Ward . | . | . | . | 29 |
| G. O. Allen, l.b.w., b. O'Reilly . | . | . | . | 9 |
| Hardstaff, b. McCormick . | . | . | . | 26 |
| Verity, not out. . | . | . | . | 0 |
| Extras (b. 8, l.b. 8, n.b. 4, w. 1) . | . | . | . | 21 |

Total (for 6 wickets) . . . . 426

Innings declared closed.

Did not bat.—R. W. V. Robins, Voce, Sims.

England first-innings bowling analysis

|  | O. | M. | R. | W. |
|---|---|---|---|---|
| McCormick . . | 20 | 1 | 79 | 2 |
| Sievers . . . | 16·2 | 4 | 30 | 0 |
| Ward . . . | 42 | 8 | 132 | 2 |
| O'Reilly . . | 41 | 17 | 86 | 1 |
| Chipperfield . . | 13 | 2 | 47 | 0 |
| McCabe . . | 9 | 1 | 31 | 1 |

Fall of the wickets:

| 1 | 2 | 3 | 4 | 5 | 6 |
|---|---|---|---|---|---|
| 27 | 118 | 247 | 351 | 368 | 424 |

## AUSTRALIA First Innings

| | |
|---|---|
| J. H. Fingleton, c. Verity, b. Voce . . . | 12 |
| L. P. O'Brien, c. Sims, b. Voce . . . . | 0 |
| D. G. Bradman, c. Allen, b. Voce . . . | 0 |
| S. J. McCabe, c. Sims, b. Voce . . . . | 0 |
| A. G. Chipperfield, c. Sims, b. Allen . . . | 13 |
| M. Sievers, c. Voce, b. Verity . . . | 4 |
| W. A. Oldfield, b. Verity . . . . . | 1 |
| W. J. O'Reilly, not out . . . . | 37 |
| E. L. McCormick, b. Allen . . . . | 10 |
| F. Ward, b. Allen . . . . . . | 0 |
| C. L. Badcock, absent ill . . . . | 0 |
| Extras (b. 1, l.b. 1, n.b. 1) . . . . | 3 |
| Total . . . . . . | 80 |

Australia first-innings bowling analysis

|  | O. | M. | R. | W. |
|---|---|---|---|---|
| Voce . . . | 8 | 1 | 10 | 4 |
| Allen . . . | 5·7 | 1 | 19 | 3 |
| Verity . . . | 3 | 0 | 17 | 2 |
| Hammond . . | 4 | 0 | 6 | 0 |
| Sims . . . | 2 | 0 | 20 | 0 |
| Robins . . . | 1 | 0 | 5 | 0 |

Fall of the wickets:

| 1 | 2 | 3 | 4 | 5 | 6 | 7 | 8 | 9 |
|---|---|---|---|---|---|---|---|---|
| 1 | 1 | 1 | 16 | 28 | 30 | 31 | 80 | 80 |

## AUSTRALIA Second Innings

| | |
|---|---:|
| J. H. Fingleton, b. Sims . . . . . | 73 |
| L. P. O'Brien, c. Allen, b. Hammond . . | 17 |
| D. G. Bradman, b. Verity . . . . . | 82 |
| S. J. McCabe, l.b.w., b. Voce . . . | 93 |
| A. G. Chipperfield, b. Voce . . . . | 21 |
| C. L. Badcock, l.b.w., b. Allen . . . . | 2 |
| M. Sievers, run out . . . . . | 24 |
| W. A. Oldfield, c. Ames, b. Voce . . . | 1 |
| W. J. O'Reilly, b. Hammond . . . . | 3 |
| E. L. McCormick, l.b.w., b. Hammond . . | 0 |
| F. Ward, not out . . . . . . | 1 |
| Extras (l.b. 3, n.b. 4) . . . | 7 |
| Total . . . . . | 324 |

Australia second-innings bowling analysis

| | O. | M. | R. | W. |
|---|---|---|---|---|
| Voce . . . | 19 | 4 | 66 | 3 |
| Allen . . . | 19 | 4 | 61 | 1 |
| Hammond . . | 15·7 | 3 | 29 | 3 |
| Sims . . . | 17 | 0 | 80 | 1 |
| Verity . . . | 19 | 7 | 55 | 1 |
| Robins . . . | 7 | 0 | 26 | 0 |

Fall of the wickets:

| 1 | 2 | 3 | 4 | 5 | 6 | 7 | 8 | 9 | 10 |
|---|---|---|---|---|---|---|---|---|---|
| 38 | 162 | 186 | 220 | 226 | 318 | 319 | 323 | 323 | 324 |

John Stuart Mill argued that on another planet two and two might easily make five; as I saw the ease of Bradman's and Fingleton's play in the first overs of the morning, and the docility of the pitch and of the bowling, I felt a weird sense of being in another dimension, where the winning side was really the losing side, seen upside down in a grotesque ironic mirror. Neither Allen nor Voce could compel the ball to rise bail-high; the position obviously was that a total of 500 or more could be gathered at leisure, given only the skill; no outside interference threatened to embarrass technique and cool thinking. Allen tried both ends of the wicket, and his energies were heroic. If determination could have knocked all three stumps into splinters, every ball from Allen would have made the wicket a carpenter's workshop. But the turf slept, and yesterday's nightmare for Australia had gone.

At twelve-thirty the England heavy artillery was silenced; Allen wore a worried look. He called up Sims, and with his fourth ball Sims beat and bowled Fingleton. It was a ball in a thousand; Sims never bowled another like it all the tour. It pitched on the leg, and hit the top of the off stump. The downfall of Fingleton was shocking in its suddenness; he had looked as sound and permanent as a public monument. Sims bowled well; he worried Bradman, who hit to the off dangerously once. McCabe, too, found in Sims cause for contemplation; a fine top-spinner almost trapped him l.b.w. Sims this morning and Sims yesterday were entirely different cricketers, the difference being that to-day the ball seemed related to his arm and fingers, and not to a sort of loose artificial limb.

When Bradman was 73 he was again morally out; a grand outswinger by Voce defeated him all the way, and only a snick saved his off stump by an inch. Voce rightly called on the high heavens. Bradman's innings was pure duty; he was often making orthodox strokes. I did not expect at any time a big score from him. Verity bowled him just before one o'clock with a short ball, nearly a long-hop, which Bradman tried to pull. Somehow his feet and whole anatomy got out of poise. This was luck for England, though England had several times rooted out Bradman's fallibility. Bradman's innings lasted nearly three hours. And so, in one quick turn of the wheel, the match was

England's again; the swing round astonished all of us, for at the day's outset England seemed doomed to long hours of labour in a batsman's paradise and eternity. Allen no doubt breathed again—I know that I did. McCabe and Chipperfield defended seriously for a considerable period; frankly I was not particularly interested hereabout in their academic proceedings. A burst of death-or-glory hitting might have led to more purposeful ends; as I watched the Australian innings now, I thought of the hen that has had its head chopped off, and runs 100 yards or so under the pathetic delusion that it is still alive.

Shortly after two-thirty Voce bowled Chipperfield; he had assisted the anti-climax for an hour. Then came Badcock from the sick room, and I thought of Eddie Paynter, of Lancashire, my distant country, deep maybe in winter, but genial with Christmas fires and good cheer. Poor Badcock did his best for a quarter of an hour before he played sadly late at Allen. So far McCabe, the cavalier, had been wearing the chilly starch of the puritan. He threw away the unnatural disguise as soon as Sievers joined him, and his innings at last became hot with challenge and fiery defiance. He hit 12 from an over by Voce, and the Hill rose from the dead. When McCabe makes a cut, or a drive, there is a flashing light and grace in it which no other Australian batsman can give us. Heavens! What would have happened to the English bowlers had Bradman not finished his heaving pull to a wretched long-hop before the said wretched long-hop arrived at its destination?

Sievers was all cold, disdainful deportment as he defended, while McCabe put grand batsmanship into the match. McCabe's strokes grew more and more luminous. He leaned forward to over-tossed off-side bowling, and through the covers the drives rippled. He cut late and fluently; his flicks to leg were the last word in polish and concealed power. At his best McCabe is one of the game's few artist batsmen—not a run-machine, but a player, who, through a game, can delight the sense of art. At tea, McCabe and Sievers were still unbeaten, with the weather again telling of rain. Destiny seemed ready to bandage eyes sardonically, and for England tantalizingly. After tea, thank goodness, Voce achieved a spell of noble effort. In the declining light he bowled beautifully at a good pace and length. He was granted a ripe reward, for McCabe tried to hook and was out leg before. McCabe palpably expected a ball with a higher rise from the ground, and seemed amazed at his end. The gallant sixth-wicket stand lasted nearly an hour and a half; it told us that the old Australian temper in a rearguard action is not yet changed to mild compliance. McCabe's innings, after a repressed prelude, was cricket at its most skilful, courtly, and chivalrous.

Shortly after McCabe left us, the patient, worthy Sievers was run out. Oldfield played a ball from Hammond to backward point, and sped like the wind. Barnett's return was prompt, and Ames did the rest. Ames is a good wicket-keeper, who does his work without advertising flourish or hullabaloo. Now the situation was in O'Reilly's hands. A lovely running-away ball from Voce found the edge of Oldfield's bat, and he would have been the first man in the world to appreciate Ames's catch at the wicket. And so O'Reilly could do little or nothing. On the heart-breaking wicket, England did very well and Australia only moderately well. We were uplifted in time for Christmas. The streets of Sydney, in the sudden and gorgeous twilight, twinkled welcome as we reached the city after the second victory. In the crowded lounge of Usher's, a man came up to me and asked if I would have a drink. I thought it was very nice of him to be so quick with his congratulations. But apparently he was celebrating for another cause. 'You are Neville Cardus', he said, and when I said I was, he went on: 'Well, here's to you. I've been looking for years for an uglier man than me, and you win easily.'

# CHAPTER X

# IRONY AT MELBOURNE

On Christmas Eve we all gave presents to Allen and congratulated him 'in advance', though there was always the thought of Bradman in our minds. The jubilation in England, telegraphed to us, rather damped our high spirits; it was the optimism which breeds trouble. The team was never really good enough to beat Australia in Australia; as one or two of the English players said: 'We are getting away with it'. The happy Christmas was a Mephistophelian preparation for the disillusionment of the New Year. On Christmas Eve I stood on the rocky edge called the 'Gap', looking towards the sea. I saw the *Awatea* sail through the Heads, glowing with rosy lights. The moon was a feather, and the Southern Cross a symbol of the night and the season of the year. I thought, as I looked at the *Awatea*: 'According to our present plans we leave Australia next March for New Zealand, homeward bound, on that same ship. Shall we really take the Ashes with us?' A few days afterwards I could give the answer; Melbourne was prophetic enough.

This was a cruel match; for on the first day England got six Australian batsmen out, all the best, for 181, on a true pitch. Then, in the night, rain made the worst wicket seen even at Melbourne in a lifetime. Hugh Trumble vowed he had never known a worse one. To me, the behaviour of the ball on this terrible Saturday went beyond all I had expected. I could scarcely believe my eyesight, as I saw the ball's preposterous behaviour. It described all manner of angles and curves; it was here, there, everywhere, spitting, darting, fizzing; now rising so abruptly that Oldfield had to hurl himself upward like a goal-keeper; now shooting and hitting Oldfield's boots. One good-length ball would rear to the batsman's chin; another, exactly the same length, would flash into the blockhole like a stone skimming over ice. A half-volley removed Ames's cap—the poor man was bereft; he ran the bye to Verity's call, not altogether knowing where he was, and then the umpire walked from square-leg and gave Ames his cap. I have never before laughed so much at a cricket match. Ames received twenty-six balls and did not get his bat within a foot of one of them. Sievers, a commonplace bowler, was unplayable. An eloquent tale is told of this Melbourne wicket by the fact that Sievers, in spite of his five for twenty-one, was not asked to play in the rubber again. Such a wicket is not known in England, for on English wickets, even at their worst, the rise of the ball is usually related to the flight through the air.

Shortly after half-past four on this crucial Saturday England were 56 for two, in reply to Australia's 200 for nine (declared). The pitch was growing fiercer and fiercer every over. Thanks to Hammond, England were marvellously not all out for 30. The question is—and everybody asked it, most of us 'after the event'—why did Allen not declare when Hammond departed, at quarter to five? The chance was there to get Bradman out for next to nothing; I doubt if any Australian batsman could have stayed in ten minutes. And of course Allen had already seen, at Brisbane and at Sydney, how feeble was Australian batsmanship on soft wickets, easy wickets compared with this one. I believe that Allen was urged by members of the English team to close the innings as soon as Hammond got out. I confess that in the Press box the idea did not at once occur to all of us; but

in the whirl of excitement—we wrote surrounded by the
raging multitude—clear thinking was not easy. My own
view was that rain was at hand any moment; as a fact, rain
did occur before close of play. Suppose that Allen had declared at a quarter to five, 140 behind. And suppose showers
had then made the turf easy. I am trying to put the case for
Allen; the weather was unsettled, and apart from immediate
expectations of more rain, there was the week-end to take
for granted. Sunday turned beautifully fine and dried the
pitch; but Allen could not foresee that. Weather in Melbourne is as treacherous as any I have ever known. It is
true that the English 'tail' seemed to throw their wickets
away, after Hammond had gone; Allen was caught in a
difficult position which called for the daring gambler's
throw of a MacLaren. He is not to be blamed for a compromise, even if it lost the rubber. Had Allen declared at a
quarter to five, Bradman would have had to send in his best
batsmen, himself included, while the roller was exercising a
merely academic influence. A sad day for English cricket,
and cruel luck for Allen to suffer! Hammond's innings, as I
shall shortly try to show, was a remarkable piece of technique. None the less, I have since often wondered whether
Hammond would not have done his side greater service by
a furious slashing assault on the bowlers, in the manner of
Trumper or Tyldesley. He stayed in eighty minutes and
scored 32. The old way on a 'sticky' Melbourne pitch was
to trust to one's eye and hit fours. Hammond was a wonder
of poise and balance: but in the circumstances, the classic
beauty of it had a sad ironic flavour somewhere.

# CHAPTER XI

# THIRD TEST—MELBOURNE

### *January 1–6, 1937*

---

## *FIRST DAY*

### AUSTRALIA First Innings

| | | | | |
|---|---|---|---|---|
| J. H. Fingleton, c. Sims, b. Robins | . | . | . | 38 |
| W. A. Brown, c. Ames, b. Voce. | . | . | . | 1 |
| D. G. Bradman, c. Robins, b. Verity . | . | . | . | 13 |
| K. E. Rigg, c. Verity, b. Allen . | . | . | . | 16 |
| S. J. McCabe, not out | . | . | . | 63 |
| L. S. Darling, c. Allen, b. Verity | . | . | . | 20 |
| M. Sievers, st. Ames, b. Robins . | . | . | . | 1 |
| W. A. Oldfield, not out | . | . | . | 21 |
| Extras (b. 2, l.b. 4, n.b. 2) . | . | . | . | 8 |

Total (for 6 wickets) . . . . 181

To bat.—W. J. O'Reilly, F. Ward, and L. O'B. Fleetwood-Smith.

Australia first-innings bowling analysis to date

| | O. | M. | R. | W. |
|---|---|---|---|---|
| Voce . . . | 14 | 3 | 41 | 1 |
| Allen . . . | 12 | 2 | 35 | 1 |
| Sims . . . | 9 | 1 | 35 | 0 |
| Verity . . . | 12·6 | 4 | 21 | 2 |
| Robins . . . | 7 | 0 | 31 | 2 |
| Hammond . . | 3 | 0 | 10 | 0 |

Fall of the wickets:

| 1 | 2 | 3 | 4 | 5 | 6 |
|---|---|---|---|---|---|
| 7 | 33 | 69 | 79 | 122 | 130 |

THE Melbourne ground was a great amphitheatre on this sunny first day of 1937. An enormous crowd dwarfed the sense of personal identity. It looked like a drawing by Fougasse. The field was an island green in the sunshine.

One man in the multitude carried a copy of *Aesop's Fables*, and read it between overs. A shout went forth when Bradman won the toss, and Bradman threw up his hands in joy unconcealed. The stage was ready for good sport; for deeds to make us happy or sorry, hopeful or desperate. The women began to shriek as soon as a ball was returned to the wicket. The batsman was yards inside his crease, but that did not matter. Excitement in a Test match is subjective, and always on the boil. The turf was on the slow side. Voce caused one ball to soar only because he dropped it short and exerted all the weight of his shoulders. None the less, Brown survived an over from Allen by inches. He almost got himself caught in the slips, and then played to leg just in front of Verity, who could not make the catch, in spite of an effort which totally disturbed his customary elegance of deportment and tranquillity of mind. Brown was palpably mortal and fallible. He lost his wicket through sweeping his bat across a not exceptionally hostile rising ball from Voce.

Bradman walked slowly to the wicket amid a roar which told not only of hero-worship, but almost of supplication. Here was the man to let in Australia's new year. He was nearly run out at once, and the women screamed and clutched one another for support. Their howls, as Mrs. Gamp would enigmatically say, were organs. Compared with a Test match in Australia, the Lancashire and York-shire match is like the Oaks after Derby Day. Bradman, I thought, was in form; a huge pull expressed the old temper. I felt that he was coming into his own at last. And with Fingleton steady and patient as usual, the Australian innings began to emerge from the amorphous. At the end of fifty minutes the score was 33.

Verity came on, and set his field thoughtfully. His first

ball travelled simply and leisurely with his arm across Bradman's pads, and Bradman obligingly gave a pretty little catch to Robins at short leg. Perhaps the ball lifted slightly, but oh what a way to get the great man out! I said to myself: 'England must win the rubber at once!' I could not believe that this incredible good fortune could blow much longer England's way. I trembled at it. Bradman, as I say, seemed ready to bring his guns into action, swift and ruthless. Gloom and inhibition returned to Australia's innings.

The boundary probably seemed located on the horizon in the eyes of Rigg and Fingleton. Full liberty was given to Sims and Verity to bowl slow to a close field. At a quarter-past one, the first four of the day was pushed by Rigg, and the crowd greeted it with the gratitude of a besieged city on being relieved. Rigg gave hints of amiable aggression. On the whole, though, I could not recognize this tame, feminine batting as Australian at all. No doubt, the bowling was steady. There was no force in the opposition to make it anything but steady. Flattery was once more being laid on with the trowel. It was all unreal, and I could not believe, and did not believe, that Australia would go on much longer in this docile way. Even the running between the wickets suggested hungry men starving to death for crumbs of singles. Rigg came terribly near to his end with the first ball sent to him by Robins—a lovely leg-spinner. He edged it in a position of body which made a combined mark of interrogation and exclamation. Fingleton at least did play more or less dependably, and so lunch came with no further cause in the crowd for dejection.

After lunch, which, by the hospitality of the Victoria Cricket Club, ceased for once in a way to be a technical term on a cricket field and became elaborately gastronomical, the match proceeded quietly for a quarter of an hour, while the great organs of the human digestion did their silent and complicated work. It was interesting to watch through glasses the faces and general demeanour of the players. Verity stood meditatively at short leg, the sun shining on his forehead, making luminous his temples of abstract thinking; Hammond, with legs astride, in the slips, unconscious of his own grace; Ames, behind the wicket while Allen walked slowly to his bowling place, often appearing to utter jokes to Hammond; Sims, in the slips, talking to everybody, beginning with Sims; Robins, at mid-off, eager and always in the game—all of them apparently unaware that thousands of packed humanity were watching them.

For a quarter of an hour, little or nothing occurred. Then Rigg, like Brown, swept his bat irrationally at a quick rising ball, and with his mouth making a round O of disgust, he saw himself beautifully caught by Verity at fine leg. An over or two afterwards, the faithful Fingleton got out. He tried to hit a four—such is human vanity—but merely landed a long-hop comfortably to cover. Sad cricket, and not fit for the grand setting on a day of Australian summer, warm and delicious to feel.

The doldrums of the afternoon suffered no interruption until Hammond bowled and slipped and fell, while bringing his arm over. This was the first occasion in the history of cricket that Hammond had been seen in an ungraceful attitude. Then Darling missed decapitating an umpire by a hair's-breadth, but these incidents were isolated in time and space. Generally the match was static. Even McCabe was kept on the defensive, and he collaborated with the accurate but, on the easy wicket, not perilous bowling. I felt the spirit of defeatism in the Australian ranks. I thought, in fact, the rubber was ours now. A fine late cut by McCabe off Hammond came as a relief to tired eyes. For quite a while, Darling stayed with McCabe, trying to make up his mind whether or not to get out, and at last he succumbed to a half-hit and a dexterous high catch at mid-off.

Verity was treated as though he were bowling at Lancashire on a sticky wicket. McCabe, a shadow of his own brilliant self, allowed a long-hop from Sims to force him back on his wicket. The batting left me, in company with 89,999 other people, astonished, dismayed, and disappointed. Sievers was stumped immediately after tea, performing a stroke which it was difficult to place in any category. At last McCabe hit Voce superbly to leg, and Oldfield obtained two fours, creating a riot amongst the women. Also, he was missed in the slips off Robins by Voce.

Dark clouds climbed the sky. Australia should by now have been in a happy position. Loose bowling by Sims helped Australia's total considerably. McCabe, though far from his best, could not altogether deny his powers of hitting. This stuff was cheap at half a crown an over. I cannot imagine why Verity was not trusted entirely with the slow part of the attack after tea. Suddenly a fall of rain dispersed the crowd, reduced the serried ranks to confusion and a temporary lack of interest in cricket. Just before five o'clock the players left the field, and did not come back. The rain descended steadily, and I walked back to my hotel, through the beautiful gardens near the ground, feeling an increase of depression. Since infancy I had heard of Melbourne's sticky wicket.

## SECOND DAY

### AUSTRALIA First Innings

| | |
|---|---:|
| J. H. Fingleton, c. Sims, b. Robins | 38 |
| W. A. Brown, c. Ames, b. Voce | 1 |
| D. G. Bradman, c. Robins, b. Verity | 13 |
| K. E. Rigg, c. Verity, b. Allen | 16 |
| S. J. McCabe, c. Worthington, b. Voce | 63 |
| L. S. Darling, c. Allen, b. Verity | 20 |
| M. Sievers, st. Ames, b. Robins | 1 |
| W. A. Oldfield, not out | 27 |
| W. J. O'Reilly, c. Sims, b. Hammond | 4 |
| F. Ward, st. Ames, b. Hammond | 7 |
| Extras (b. 2, l.b. 6, n.b. 2) | 10 |
| Total (for 9 wickets) | 200 |

Innings declared closed.

Did not bat.—L. O'B. Fleetwood-Smith.

### Australia first-innings bowling analysis

| | O. | M. | R. | W. |
|---|---:|---:|---:|---:|
| Voce | 18 | 3 | 49 | 2 |
| Allen | 12 | 2 | 35 | 1 |
| Sims | 9 | 1 | 35 | 0 |
| Verity | 14 | 4 | 24 | 2 |
| Robins | 7 | 0 | 1 | 2 |
| Hammond | 5·3 | 0 | 16 | 2 |

### Fall of the wickets:

| 1 | 2 | 3 | 4 | 5 | 6 | 7 | 8 | 9 |
|---|---|---|---|---|---|---|---|---|
| 7 | 33 | 69 | 79 | 122 | 130 | 183 | 190 | 200 |

### ENGLAND First Innings

| | |
|---|---:|
| Worthington, c. Bradman, b. McCabe | 0 |
| Barnett, c. Darling, b. Sievers | 11 |
| Hammond, c. Darling, b. Sievers | 32 |
| Leyland, c. Darling, b. O'Reilly | 17 |
| Sims, c. Brown, b. Sievers | 3 |
| Ames, b. Sievers | 3 |
| R. W. V. Robins, c. O'Reilly, b. Sievers | 0 |
| Hardstaff, b. O'Reilly | 3 |

ENGLAND First Innings—*continued*

| | | | | | | |
|---|---|---|---|---|---|---|
| G. O. Allen, not out | . | . | . | . | . | o |
| Verity, c. Brown, b. O'Reilly | . | . | . | . | o |
| Extras (b. 5, l.b. 1, n.b. 1) . | | . | . | . | 7 |

Total (for 9 wickets) .   .   .   . 76

Innings declared closed.

Did not bat.—Voce.

England first-innings bowling analysis

| | O. | M. | R. | W. |
|---|---|---|---|---|
| McCabe     .   . | 2 | 1 | 7 | 1 |
| Sievers .   .   . | 11·2 | 5 | 21 | 5 |
| O'Reilly     .   . | 12 | 5 | 28 | 3 |
| Fleetwood-Smith . | 3 | 1 | 13 | o |

Fall of the wickets:

| 1 | 2 | 3 | 4 | 5 | 6 | 7 | 8 | 9 |
|---|---|---|---|---|---|---|---|---|
| o | 14 | 56 | 68 | 71 | 71 | 76 | 76 | 76 |

AUSTRALIA Second Innings

| | | | | | | |
|---|---|---|---|---|---|---|
| W. J. O'Reilly, c. and b. Voce . | | . | . | . | . | o |
| L. O'B. Fleetwood-Smith, not out | | . | . | . | o |
| F. Ward, not out   . | . | . | . | . | . | 1 |
| Extras (n.b. 2) . | | . | . | . | . | 2 |

Total (for 1 wicket) .   .   .   . 3

In an atmosphere of expectancy, the match was resumed after lunch. At once the wicket began to amuse itself and the crowd, and possibly the England bowlers, though their pleasure must have been rather mixed. In Voce's first over, in which the ball kicked, putting an end to McCabe's innings, Worthington took the inevitable catch almost under protest. O'Reilly was received with a convulsion of laughter. The first ball to him stood up and stared him in the face. He patted the wicket masterfully, and really it deserved all the smacking it got. Verity bowled only an over or two, and then gave way to Hammond. It was, so far, a jumping rather than a turning wicket. A stylish catch by Sims in the slips completed the comedy act by O'Reilly. This was another nasty rising ball, which it gave me no delight to see.

We knew already that on such a playful stretch of turf Australia's total could easily be a winning one. Bradman closed the innings when Ward was stumped, and Oldfield deservedly carried out his brave bat. His innings had been marked by cleverness.

The crowd tasted English blood without delay. McCabe's third ball came up, as though jerked by invisible elastic, to the top of Worthington's bat. He was formally caught at silly point, amid howls of joy. McCabe then thumped Hammond's glove. If McCabe is able to achieve angles on a wicket, then the reputation of that wicket must be beyond argument. Barnett smote the beast savagely. Sutcliffe used to deal more soothingly with a Melbourne sticky pitch. He coaxed it, and, like a faithful gardener, took his time over it. Barnett drove McCabe for a desperate four, received the next ball on his arm, beat the earth again, and thumped a two to the on, while the crowd smacked lips and looked for a wicket every over.

O'Reilly attacked, instead of McCabe, and Hammond obtained two through the slips from a defensive push forward, scientifically correct in the abstract, but entirely uncontrolled on this most unscientific wicket. One ball from O'Reilly rose straight from a good length to Hammond's cap. J. T. Tyldesley once told me of the sprightly terrors of the Melbourne pitch after rain, and now I have seen it I am at a loss to account for his mastery on it—and Victor Trumper's—against great bowling.

Barnett in vain tried to escape from his trap. He hooked Sievers, and the stroke went up like the lark ascending; the Australians gathered together conversationally, and one or two of them indulged in playful catching with the ball. Leyland then drove O'Reilly for a four, which was a good Yorkshire stroke; and Hammond thrust out his left leg, and hit Sievers to the off so beautifully that he momentarily created the illusion of a fast, smooth lawn.

I was lost in amazement and admiration of the way Hammond continued in the gyrating circumstances to maintain something of his own poise and reasonableness. He was like a cool, cultivated surveyor applying a spirit level in a volcanic region.

Frankly, Australia were not bowling too well for the situation's needs. Against Trumble and Saunders 50 all out would, I fancy, have taxed the batsmen severely, between three and four o'clock. Never before had I, or anybody else, seen a wicket so spiteful and eccentric.

At half-past four England were incredibly 56 for two, which was equal to 156 on a respectable honest turf. Leyland fell in the endeavour to pull a ball which shot upwards. He merely glanced it, and Darling on the leg side took a glorious falling catch, swift as the bird of prey. A real sticky-wicket catch. Leyland for forty minutes was an experienced Yorkshireman, using his bat resolutely, and the whole extent of his body. His bruises were spectacular the next day.

Meanwhile Hammond went his way, revealing himself for the time being as the world's greatest batsman, fair weather and foul. Fleetwood-Smith spun abruptly with a length that fluctuated between long-hop, good occasional length, and poly-hop. I suffered a crick in the neck hereabout, contemplating the gathering clouds. Allen also was obviously hoping for relieving torrents, because he sent Sims in at the fall of the third wicket.

At a quarter to five Hammond was out, or rather dethroned. Sievers kicked viciously into his bat, and another brilliant tumbling catch by Darling changed a protective stab into a fatal one. Pandemonium broke loose. Hammond was given magnificent applause, and he deserved it. None the less, the great note in the crowd's roar was exultant. England were surely at the last gasp now. There was a shriek at every ball. When Fingleton leaped up, like Nijinsky, at an attempt to catch Ames, I feared my eardrums would split. And with Hammond out of the way, the bowling took on the accuracy that was the only thing needed. Sievers became deadly, such was the wicket's transforming power. Sims played him mainly with breastbone, and perhaps that was as good a way as any.

Sims at last made the mistake of using his bat, and another nimble catch near the wicket, this time by Brown, settled him. The crowd vociferously began to count England out, and they could scarcely keep in time. Sievers took three wickets in an over. The scorers obtained the necessary particulars, as one after the other the victims came to the slaughter. There was no ignominy in the collapse. The wicket was beyond the reach of a normal batting technique. Sievers does not make a habit of getting three wickets in an over. But he earned his successes, for he had the sense to keep a length.

Allen declared at last—anxious to give Australia a taste, after all, of the afternoon's horrors. It seemed a grim belated joke, as well as strategy hopeful and embarrassed and enforced.

## *THIRD DAY*

### AUSTRALIA First Innings

| | |
|---|---|
| J. H. Fingleton, c. Sims, b. Robins . . . | 38 |
| W. A. Brown, c. Ames, b. Voce . . . | 1 |
| D. G. Bradman, c. Robins, b. Verity . . . | 13 |
| K. E. Rigg, c. Verity, b. Allen . . . . | 16 |
| S. J. McCabe, c. Worthington, b. Voce . . | 63 |
| L. S. Darling, c. Allen, b. Verity . . . | 20 |
| M. Sievers, st. Ames, b. Robins . . . . | 1 |
| W. A. Oldfield, not out . . . . . | 27 |
| W. J. O'Reilly, c. Sims, b. Hammond . . | 4 |
| F. Ward, st. Ames, b. Hammond . . . | 7 |
| Extras (b. 2, l.b. 6, n.b. 2) . . . . | 10 |

Total (for 9 wickets) . . . . 200
Innings declared closed.
Did not bat.—L. O'B. Fleetwood-Smith.

### Australia first-innings bowling analysis

| | O. | M. | R. | W. |
|---|---|---|---|---|
| Voce . . . | 18 | 3 | 49 | 2 |
| Allen . . . | 12 | 2 | 35 | 1 |
| Sims . . . | 9 | 1 | 35 | 0 |
| Verity . . . | 14 | 4 | 24 | 2 |
| Robins . . . | 7 | 0 | 1 | 2 |
| Hammond . . | 5·3 | 0 | 16 | 2 |

### Fall of the wickets:

| 1 | 2 | 3 | 4 | 5 | 6 | 7 | 8 | 9 |
|---|---|---|---|---|---|---|---|---|
| 7 | 33 | 69 | 79 | 122 | 130 | 183 | 190 | 200 |

### ENGLAND First Innings

| | |
|---|---|
| Worthington, c. Bradman, b. McCabe . . | 0 |
| Barnett, c. Darling, b. Sievers . . . | 11 |
| Hammond, c. Darling, b. Sievers . . . | 32 |
| Leyland, c. Darling, b. O'Reilly . . . | 17 |
| Sims, c. Brown, b. Sievers . . . . | 3 |
| Ames, b. Sievers . . . . . . | 3 |
| R. W. V. Robins, c. O'Reilly, b. Sievers . . | 0 |
| Hardstaff, b. O'Reilly . . . . | 3 |
| G. O. Allen, not out . . . . . | 0 |
| Verity, c. Brown, b. O'Reilly . . . . | 0 |
| Extras (b. 5, l.b. 1, n.b. 1) . . . | 7 |

Total (for 9 wickets) . . . . 76
Innings declared closed.
Did not bat.—Voce.

England first-innings bowling analysis

|  | O. | M. | R. | W. |
|---|---|---|---|---|
| McCabe . . | 2 | 1 | 7 | 1 |
| Sievers . . . | 11·2 | 5 | 21 | 5 |
| O'Reilly . . | 12 | 5 | 28 | 3 |
| Fleetwood-Smith . | 3 | 1 | 13 | 0 |

Fall of the wickets:

| 1 | 2 | 3 | 4 | 5 | 6 | 7 | 8 | 9 |
|---|---|---|---|---|---|---|---|---|
| 0 | 14 | 56 | 68 | 71 | 71 | 76 | 76 | 76 |

### AUSTRALIA SECOND INNINGS

| | |
|---|---|
| W. J. O'Reilly, c. and b. Voce . . . . | 0 |
| L. O'B. Fleetwood-Smith, c. Verity, b. Voce . | 0 |
| F. Ward, c. Hardstaff, b. Verity . . . | 18 |
| K. E. Rigg, l.b.w. (n.), b. Sims . . . . | 47 |
| W. A. Brown, c. Barnett, b. Voce . . . | 20 |
| J. H. Fingleton, not out . . . . . | 39 |
| D. G. Bradman, not out . . . . . | 56 |
| Extras (b. 5, l.b. 1, n.b. 8) . . . . | 14 |
| Total (for 5 wickets) . . . . | 194 |

Australia second-innings bowling analysis to date

|  | O. | M. | R. | W. |
|---|---|---|---|---|
| Voce . . . | 17 | 2 | 66 | 3 |
| Hammond . . | 8 | 1 | 22 | 0 |
| Allen . . . | 7 | 1 | 23 | 0 |
| Verity . . . | 8 | 1 | 15 | 1 |
| Robins . . . | 2 | 0 | 8 | 0 |
| Sims . . . | 8 | 0 | 33 | 1 |
| Worthington . . | 3 | 0 | 13 | 0 |

Fall of the wickets:

| 1 | 2 | 3 | 4 | 5 |
|---|---|---|---|---|
| 0 | 3 | 38 | 74 | 97 |

To win back a position lost on an unplayable pitch England needed not only superb cricket, but a generous compensation from fortune, after the sport of Saturday. Rain helped England at Brisbane and Sydney, no doubt. Allen could now say that he had had the worst of the throw of the dice. The 'gluepot' of Melbourne was evil enough to tackle in itself. To-day, when there was still a bare prospect of an England rally on a transformed turf, showers came even as England's bowlers appeared ready to do their best, and after Australia had lost five wickets for 97.

There was again a mighty crowd waiting for the blood and thunder. A policeman guarded the wicket. It was really his duty to arrest the wretch for disturbing the peace. Voce's third ball soared upwards, and Fleetwood-Smith hastily departed, while the England team inspected the turf, tenderly pressing fingers into it, like doctors searching for appendicitis. Ward was missed in the slips, off Voce, by Sims; but it quickly became apparent that the wicket, compared with Saturday's infamy, was a reformed, not to say a repentant character, for though Voce could obtain for a while a vital rise from the ground, it could be usually deduced from the flight and length. At the other end Allen could be more or less rationally played. A good batsman now had at least a chance to apply a normal technique. Even Ward was able to use the middle of his bat, and if Rigg once received a breakback from Allen on the behind it was because he preferred to apply his behind rather than his bat. At a quarter to one the batsmen were at liberty to watch the quick bowlers with time to spare.

It now seemed that the most delicate art of Verity would be needed by England to make any considerable advance. No longer was the pitch eager to lend terrors to a long-hop. Allen even asked Robins to try his hand, a dangerous experiment, I thought, considering that England could not afford to give a single run away. Ward stayed in an hour to-day, as orthodox as a book. He was caught by Hardstaff running back at mid-on (from a hit which deceptively hinted of spin in Verity's allurements).

Allen trusted Robins with only one over. Voce was

called back as soon as Brown took guard. England's plan of attack now was surely accuracy at one end, Hammond and Voce in turn, while Verity did his best at the other. But over by over the turf improved under the cloudy sky. Saturday's nightmare was gone. The batsmen could safely turn Verity to leg for singles, a sad sign. England's only hope seemed to be for a continuance of the fine weather, for a good roller, for a thoroughly easy wicket for the fourth innings, and for Hammond in his pomp.

England did not do well enough before lunch. Fleet-wood-Smith and Ward were a poor bag in ninety minutes. Voce and Verity pitched too short, and Allen not short enough. After the interval the crowd was massive, and again the women let out shrieks at every attempt at a safe, if short run. Brown succumbed to one of Voce's short lengths, which, by accident more than design, encouraged his hook. Barnett calculated the catch nicely. Rigg began to play neat cricket. I liked his general air of confidence and alertness, though Sims totally beat him when he was 42 with one of the first well-flighted balls he bowled. Too few balls drew the batsmen forward, and Rigg rightly plundered a four, all run, from a long-hop by Verity. Whenever Sims found a spacious length he gave trouble, and he got rid of Rigg with a most charming spinner. And so Bradman arrived, Australia 221 ahead, and half the side out, the game's point of crisis. Everything depended on Bradman, and he knew it. Sims discovered the right curve through the air, and caused Bradman at once to change his mind. Then with the match in the scales tantalizingly, the rain played jokes, starting and stopping, so that the cricketers and umpires did not know what to do, and wandered to and from the pavilion's direction like people lost in the Hampton Court maze.

The rain at length made up its mind, and the game was interrupted. The English bowlers were no doubt glad to be rid of the wet ball, which at the peak of the turning-point was hindering their skill. Yet the advent of rain was a terrible menace to England's remnant of a chance. With cruel waywardness the shower passed, and Voce, grappling with wet soap and sawdust, was hit for 13 in five balls by Bradman at his fiercest and most opportunist.

Bradman's crashing assault seemed like the knock out for England, and rain again caused a run to the pavilion, full speed, glad to be rid of another scurvy buffeting from the gods. When Bradman came in, Australia had done none too well by scoring 97 for five on a wicket good enough for any good batsman. The spin of Sims suggested possibilities. But no man can spin slippery leather, or keep a length with it. Allen's emotions were probably mixed. If the rain ceased, his bowlers would be flogged. If it persisted, there would be another holocaust in the morning. A side cannot fight back with the weather a turncock and a rogue. Poor Allen, scourged after so much apparent good will from the gods!

### FOURTH DAY

#### AUSTRALIA First Innings

| | |
|---|---:|
| J. H. Fingleton, c. Sims, b. Robins | 38 |
| W. A. Brown, c. Ames, b. Voce | 1 |
| D. G. Bradman, c. Robins, b. Verity | 13 |
| K. E. Rigg, c. Verity, b. Allen | 16 |
| S. J. McCabe, c. Worthington, b. Voce | 63 |
| L. S. Darling, c. Allen, b. Verity | 20 |
| M. Sievers, st. Ames, b. Robins | 1 |
| W. A. Oldfield, not out | 27 |
| W. J. O'Reilly, c. Sims, b. Hammond | 4 |
| F. Ward, st. Ames, b. Hammond | 7 |
| Extras (b. 2, l.b. 6, n.b. 2) | 10 |
| Total (for 9 wickets) | 200 |

Innings declared closed.
Did not bat.—L. O'B. Fleetwood-Smith.

### Australia first-innings bowling analysis

|          | O.   | M. | R. | W. |
|----------|------|----|----|----|
| Voce     | 18   | 3  | 49 | 2  |
| Allen    | 12   | 2  | 35 | 1  |
| Sims     | 9    | 1  | 35 | 0  |
| Verity   | 14   | 4  | 24 | 2  |
| Robins   | 7    | 0  | 31 | 2  |
| Hammond  | 5·3  | 0  | 16 | 2  |

### Fall of the wickets:

| 1 | 2  | 3  | 4  | 5   | 6   | 7   | 8   | 9   |
|---|----|----|----|-----|-----|-----|-----|-----|
| 7 | 33 | 69 | 79 | 122 | 130 | 183 | 190 | 200 |

### ENGLAND First Innings

| | |
|---|---|
| Worthington, c. Bradman, b. McCabe | 0 |
| Barnett, c. Darling, b. Sievers | 11 |
| Hammond, c. Darling, b. Sievers | 32 |
| Leyland, c. Darling, b. O'Reilly | 17 |
| Sims, c. Brown, b. Sievers | 3 |
| Ames, b. Sievers | 3 |
| R. W. V. Robins, c. O'Reilly, b. Sievers | 0 |
| Hardstaff, b. O'Reilly | 3 |
| G. O. Allen, not out | 0 |
| Verity, c. Brown, b. O'Reilly | 0 |
| Extras (b. 5, l.b. 1, n.b. 1) | 7 |
| Total (for 9 wickets) | 76 |

Innings declared closed.
Did not bat.—Voce.

### England first-innings bowling analysis

|                 | O.    | M. | R. | W. |
|-----------------|-------|----|----|----|
| McCabe          | 2     | 1  | 7  | 1  |
| Sievers         | 11·2  | 5  | 21 | 5  |
| O'Reilly        | 12    | 5  | 28 | 3  |
| Fleetwood-Smith | 5     | 1  | 13 | 0  |

### Fall of the wickets:

| 1 | 2  | 3  | 4  | 5  | 6  | 7  | 8  | 9  |
|---|----|----|----|----|----|----|----|----|
| 0 | 14 | 56 | 68 | 71 | 71 | 76 | 76 | 76 |

## AUSTRALIA Second Innings

| | |
|---|---:|
| W. J. O'Reilly, c. and b. Voce | 0 |
| L. O'B. Fleetwood-Smith, c. Verity, b. Voce | 0 |
| F. Ward, c. Hardstaff, b. Verity | 18 |
| K. E. Rigg, l.b.w. (n.), b. Sims | 47 |
| W. A. Brown, c. Barnett, b. Voce | 20 |
| J. H. Fingleton, c. Ames, b. Sims | 136 |
| D. G. Bradman, not out | 248 |
| S. J. McCabe, not out | 14 |
| Extras (b. 6, l.b. 2, n.b. 9) | 17 |
| Total (for 6 wickets) | 500 |

Australia second-innings bowling analysis to date

| | O. | M. | R. | W. |
|---|---|---|---|---|
| Voce | 29 | 2 | 120 | 3 |
| Hammond | 21 | 3 | 82 | 0 |
| Allen | 17 | 2 | 62 | 0 |
| Verity | 34 | 6 | 75 | 1 |
| Robins | 7 | 0 | 36 | 0 |
| Sims | 16 | 0 | 90 | 2 |
| Worthington | 4 | 0 | 18 | 0 |

Fall of the wickets:

| 1 | 2 | 3 | 4 | 5 | 6 |
|---|---|---|---|---|---|
| 0 | 3 | 38 | 74 | 97 | 443 |

On a rich couch stuffed with runs, Australia made victory only a matter of time. Bradman and Fingleton seized a ripe chance. In the happiest conditions for batsmen, rare skill is required to sustain a stand of nearly a day's duration. And England's attack was as good as heartbreaking turf could allow any attack to be that did not contain a Barnes or a Larwood.

Verity was magnificent; in his absence Bradman might have scored another hundred runs. Up to a point, Bradman played at his second best. None the less his greatness was beyond argument. I never believed in his poor scores, and I was not prophetic but merely deductive when I wrote that Bradman's day was coming back, and was almost on us.

Bradman and Fingleton scored 343 together in 364 minutes, and Sims broke the partnership. He was scarcely used enough in a state of affairs which called for some humorous bowling now and then. Australia was so far ahead, and Bradman and Fingleton so thoroughly set, that a few extra runs to the growing pile would not have mattered. Sims is always likely to fool a confident player into a blunder.

It was a lovely morning for the fourth day, soft sunshine and sailing white clouds, like any summer day at Old Trafford. And again a fine crowd to see Bradman; work and all forms of manual labour are rightly dismissed from the mind by Melbourne whenever Test cricket is shaking the continent. On this morning as I left my hotel, I saw a group of little girls setting forth—armed with wickets and bats, ready for action at the first signs of failure in Australian manhood, and no doubt qualified already to join the women in the crowd and scream for Australia at the top of their voices.

Bradman and Fingleton came to the wicket, to strengthen further a strong position which nobody foresaw on Friday. The rain was the villain of the piece for England. Fortune, as I say, snatched away from Allen quite as much as she gave him at Brisbane and Sydney, where the wickets never became half as sinful as Melbourne's. But the scurviest trick served by luck to England was the drizzle which on the third afternoon reduced a confident attack to greasy impotence. A sticky wicket one day is, so to say, part of the game, to be accepted philosophically. But a slippery ball the next day . . .!

To mention these matters is not to detract from the

keen, skilful way Australia seized the chances. Here at last was much of the old hostility, the swift pounce on the broken enemy. The wicket was as easy for Bradman and Fingleton as middle-age, or vintage port. Voce could scarcely make the new ball rise knee-high, and Bradman pulled his deliveries with the familiar dynamic movement. The conditions were his ally.

Allen bowled with so great an effort that after a single ball his hair became tousled; he actually sent a ball flying past Fingleton's breastbone to the off, but this miracle was, as miracles should be, exceptional. Voce then forced Bradman back in a superb over of perfect length and rhythm. Bradman was glad to edge a fine outswinger for a single, and the next ball, a masterpiece of accurate swerve, went through the slips also behind Fingleton's back, while Fingleton was probably wondering in a flash of apprehension whether anybody had held a catch while he wasn't looking. It was easy to feel the sense of strain in the efforts of England's fast bowlers to take a wicket. Allen troubled Bradman, who was guilty of a dangerous stroke to point. The batting and the turf frustrated the onslaught, and Hammond came to the relief of Voce. It is always good captaincy to give Hammond the ball while it is still new.

Fingleton again played perpendicularly, not obviously thinking of runs, which came to him by a sort of interest on the time accumulated during his stay at the wicket. And Bradman could not unleash himself; his batting was tied to the kennel for a long time. None the less Australia was attending to the right job, grimly digging the deep hole for England's funeral.

The English attack was admirably steady, and Voce worked heroically on a wicket sent by heaven to Australia's batsmen, so soon after the shambles. The runs continued to come slowly, a by-product of the general war of attrition. Bradman's cricket was, in the term of Karl Marx, congealed labour. The gigantic crowd sunned itself in placid contentment, men, women, children; sitting, standing, craning their necks, squatting on steps, even hanging on to rails. I suppose that a number of the population of Melbourne was actually not present, but working at home, or in offices, with all their excuses worn out for the time being. In England we do not know what a Test match is, as an expression of the national consciousness.

At lunch, Bradman and Fingleton were still not out, and apparently beyond serious error. After lunch (which by the way consisted of oysters, turkey, asparagus, jelly, and trifle), Verity proceeded with his precise bowling, which before the interval cost England only seven runs in fifty-six balls. His length dropped with the persistence of water on a rock. I began to look for stalactites hanging down to the earth.

The wicket was now the best and most cosy and comfortable seen in the Test matches during the season. Bradman cut Voce brilliantly, and reached his 100, a State-Occasion effort, related to his cricket in England of six years ago as the honest mason's productions are related to architecture. But, as I say, I expected him to begin at any moment and shed his armour.

The dazzling returns of Robins produced further hysterics amongst the women. Bradman drove Sims with a grand running drive, and pulled voraciously to leg. The banked fires of his innings appeared at last to have been struck into a blaze. But Sims had the honour of beating him at least once. This was the only sign of mortality in Bradman that the England attack had witnessed for many, many persevering overs, during which the really encouraging influence to Allen was Robins's attempts to run somebody out. He seemed to cover acres of space, and cover or back up all the other fieldsmen, himself included. He was a joy to see, and you had to be quick to see him, as he flashed and swooped here, there, and everywhere.

Verity put another shovel of damp coal on Bradman's play; he worried the great man, who, even against a long-hop from Sims, now and again pulled prodigiously, and got only a single. The old genius shot out once more as soon as Allen came on at 323—a fierce off-drive from the back foot. So was England's pit deepened, and Fingleton went his ways, a good second grave-digger, who might have said that he had been on this job at this cemetery, man and boy, these many years. He does his job diligently, with a straight bat seldom lifted up higher than his knee, and he is always ready, for the cause, to contribute his share modestly, even anonymously. He deserved his sojourn on to-day's heavenly wicket, for he played a brave and lonely hand at Brisbane, and at Sydney he was also dependable, in difficult straits.

When Fingleton reached his 100 he was given roars of applause, the generous like of which I have seldom heard at a cricket match; they were prolonged, and culminated in three rousing cheers. It was the sort of ovation that the foreigners give to Toscanini after he has conducted an opera. The English team accepted the situation now with commendable philosophy, and Robins, having sought in vain to run the batsmen out, came on to bowl, also apparently for run-outs.

After tea Verity continued his artistic bowling, and twice in one over he beat Bradman. The duel between Bradman and Verity was the vital interest of the afternoon, and Verity did not emerge second best on points, as they say.

Nothing but consummate length and flight could have checked Bradman, in circumstances made for Bradman. Nowadays, all the applause is for the batsman, but the Melbourne crowd appreciated Verity's skill, and recognized it warmly after an over which Bradman needed all his wits to counter. Verity's accuracy made the position of silly point as safe as it was necessary, technically and psychologically, all day. Every run scored from Verity had to be earned. It was beautiful bowling, delightful to the eye and to the intellect.

In the hour between five and six, Bradman was helping himself, for now the attack failed from sheer weariness. Allen endeavoured to transform himself into a slow-to-medium-paced bowler; he expressed a noble disgust.

---

## FIFTH DAY

### AUSTRALIA First Innings

| | |
|---|---:|
| J. H. Fingleton, c. Sims, b. Robins | 38 |
| W. A. Brown, c. Ames, b. Voce | 1 |
| D. G. Bradman, c. Robins, b. Verity | 13 |
| K. E. Rigg, c. Verity, b. Allen | 16 |
| S. J. McCabe, c. Worthington, b. Voce | 63 |
| L. S. Darling, c. Allen, b. Verity | 20 |
| M. Sievers, st. Ames, b. Robins | 1 |
| W. A. Oldfield, not out | 27 |
| W. J. O'Reilly, c. Sims, b. Hammond | 4 |
| F. Ward, st. Ames, b. Hammond | 7 |
| Extra (b. 2, l.b. 6, n.b. 2) | 10 |

Total (for 9 wickets) . . . . 200

Innings declared closed.

Australia first-innings bowling analysis

| | O. | M. | R. | W. |
|---|---|---|---|---|
| Voce | 18 | 3 | 49 | 2 |
| Allen | 12 | 2 | 35 | 1 |
| Sims | 9 | 1 | 35 | 0 |
| Verity | 14 | 4 | 24 | 2 |
| Robins | 7 | 0 | 31 | 2 |
| Hammond | 5·3 | 0 | 16 | 2 |

Fall of the wickets:

| 1 | 2 | 3 | 4 | 5 | 6 | 7 | 8 | 9 |
|---|---|---|---|---|---|---|---|---|
| 7 | 33 | 69 | 79 | 122 | 130 | 183 | 190 | 200 |

### ENGLAND First Innings

| | |
|---|---|
| Worthington, c. Bradman, b. McCabe . . | 0 |
| Barnett, c. Darling, b. Sievers . . . | 11 |
| Hammond, c. Darling, b. Sievers . . | 32 |
| Leyland, c. Darling, b. O'Reilly. . . | 17 |
| Sims, c. Brown, b. Sievers . . . | 3 |
| Ames, b. Sievers . . . . . | 3 |
| R. W. V. Robins, c. O'Reilly, b. Sievers . . | 0 |
| Hardstaff, b. O'Reilly . . . . | 3 |
| G. O. Allen, not out . . . . | 0 |
| Verity, c. Brown, b. O'Reilly . . . | 0 |
| Extras (b. 5, l.b. 1, n.b. 1) . . . | 7 |

Total (for 9 wickets) . . . . 76

Innings declared closed.

England first-innings bowling analysis

| | O. | M. | R. | W. |
|---|---|---|---|---|
| McCabe . . | 2 | 1 | 7 | 1 |
| Sievers . . . | 11·2 | 5 | 21 | 5 |
| O'Reilly . . | 12 | 5 | 28 | 3 |
| Fleetwood-Smith . | 3 | 1 | 13 | 0 |

Fall of the wickets:

| 1 | 2 | 3 | 4 | 5 | 6 | 7 | 8 | 9 |
|---|---|---|---|---|---|---|---|---|
| 0 | 14 | 56 | 68 | 71 | 71 | 67 | 76 | 76 |

### AUSTRALIA Second Innings

| | |
|---|---|
| W. J. O'Reilly, c. and b. Voce . . . | 0 |
| L. O'B. Fleetwood-Smith, c. Verity, b. Voce . | 0 |
| F. Ward, c. Hardstaff, b. Verity . . | 18 |
| K. E. Rigg, l.b.w. (n.), b. Sims . . . | 47 |
| W. A. Brown, c. Barnett, b. Voce . . | 20 |
| J. H. Fingleton, c. Ames, b. Sims . . | 136 |
| D. G. Bradman, c. Allen, b. Verity . . | 270 |
| S. J. McCabe, l.b.w. (n.), b. Allen . . | 22 |
| L. S. Darling, b. Allen . . . . | 0 |
| W. A. Oldfield, l.b.w., b. Verity . . | 7 |
| M. Sievers, not out . . . . | 25 |
| Extras (b. 6, l.b. 2, n.b. 10, w. 1) . . | 19 |

Total . . . . . 564

Australia second-innings bowling analysis

|              | O.   | M. | R.  | W. |
|--------------|------|----|-----|----|
| Voce .   .   . | 29 | 2 | 120 | 3 |
| Hammond  .   . | 22 | 3 | 89  | 0 |
| Allen .   .   . | 23 | 2 | 84  | 2 |
| Verity .   .   . | 37·7 | 9 | 79 | 3 |
| Robins .   .   . | 11 | 2 | 46  | 0 |
| Sims .   .   . | 23 | 1 | 109 | 2 |
| Worthington . . | 4 | 0 | 18  | 0 |

Fall of the wickets:

| 1 | 2 | 3 | 4 | 5 | 6 | 7 | 8 | 9 | 10 |
|---|---|---|---|---|---|---|---|---|----|
| 0 | 3 | 38 | 74 | 97 | 443 | 511 | 511 | 549 | 564 |

### ENGLAND Second Innings

| | |
|---|---|
| Worthington, c. Sievers, b. Ward   .   .   . | 16 |
| Barnett, l.b.w., b. O'Reilly   .   .   .   . | 23 |
| Hammond, b. Sievers   .   .   .   .   . | 51 |
| Leyland, not out   .   .   .   .   .   . | 69 |
| Ames, b. Fleetwood-Smith   .   .   .   . | 19 |
| Hardstaff, c. Ward, b. Fleetwood-Smith   .   . | 17 |
| G. O. Allen, c. Sievers, b. Fleetwood-Smith   . | 11 |
| R. W. V. Robins, not out   .   .   .   . | 27 |
| Extras   .   .   .   .   .   .   . | 3 |

Total (for 6 wickets) .   .   .   . 236

England second-innings bowling analysis to date

|                  | O. | M. | R.  | W. |
|------------------|----|----|-----|----|
| Sievers .   .   . | 8  | 2  | 19  | 1  |
| McCabe   .   . | 4  | 0  | 13  | 0  |
| O'Reilly   .   . | 16 | 6  | 40  | 1  |
| Fleetwood-Smith . | 21 | 1  | 101 | 3  |
| Ward .   .   . | 12 | 1  | 60  | 1  |

Fall of the wickets:

| 1 | 2 | 3 | 4 | 5 | 6 |
|---|---|---|---|---|---|
| 29 | 65 | 117 | 155 | 179 | 195 |

When Sievers bowled Hammond after tea on the fifth day, with a ball of vivid pace from the pitch, the match was won and lost: it was of course won and lost on the sticky pitch, and the only interest in England's second innings was whether a big enough score would be made to prevent a considerable improvement of the moral composure of Australia's attack. The wicket was slightly faster than it had been on the fourth day, and for that reason not so heart-breaking for the bowlers; perhaps there were even a few spots, but if so they were as spots on the sun.

Hammond, at his most grand and leonine, again made batsmanship a natural instinct. Leyland was spasmodic, and on the whole the England second innings disappointed. But it is sorry work playing in a hopeless strait, and Australia found inspiration in the heady atmosphere of a position from which nothing could be seen but victory and all her smiles and laurels.

During the evening, after Hammond got out, a wicket or two was lost by England in a way which suggested that the players were resigned to their end and anxious only that the last kick should be a gay one; they were perhaps sensible not to prolong the agony; still, I wished that some of Hammond's and Leyland's supernumeraries would look hard for the form which had brought them out of the fogs and cold to Australia.

On the morning of this fifth day, which was warm and pleasant, at least half of the population of Melbourne had apparently returned to work, if only temporarily, and as a sign of good intentions. There were pretty clouds in the sky, and somehow the Melbourne wicket reminded me of Mr. Charles Peace, who most days in the week used to burgle and knock policemen on the head, and on Sundays go to church and play the organ. Melbourne's turf seems capable of that kind of humorous double life.

Bradman's performance meant much to the Australian team. For weeks I had been saying that it was necessary for England to win the rubber before Bradman escaped from a vein of ill-luck; our bowlers had not been beating him technically; he had been getting out to unreal, inexplicable strokes. The big score cleared the air; and at Adelaide there was, we suspected, likely to be a beautiful wicket and hot weather; 100 in the shade, and Bradman 300 in the sun. A band of brass instruments was present, and played a tune which I recognized as 'The British Grenadiers' as the English team took the field. Sims danced a hornpipe; none the less it was 'The British Grenadiers'. There was no mistaking it.

Voce was unable to play because of something wrong with an ankle, so Sims, fresh from his hornpipe, opened the attack with Allen, who at once got rid of McCabe leg before, and next ball clean bowled Darling, whose stroke was sinfully crooked. Two wickets in two balls, and on the day before one wicket in one day. This game is sardonic. Bradman was quiet for a while, and unwell. In an hour Australia scored only 49. Then Verity came on, and Bradman seemed to weary of his own inactivity; he tried to drive, skied the ball, and Allen made a clever catch facing the crowd.

At a quarter-past two England began the task or hardship of trying to score a matter of 680-odd runs; 'Dem' the ninepence,' as Mr. Mantalini would say. Worthington was promptly missed at short square leg off Sievers by Fleetwood-Smith, who probably was not expecting a catch so early in the proceedings. The wicket was still stuffed with runs; there seemed no reason why England should not bat for hours, and even if nearly 700 was a remote goal, it was England's job to put the Australian bowlers sufficiently out of countenance to send them to Adelaide not at all confident of their chances there.

Barnett drove McCabe charmingly to the off, and cut Sievers square with a pretty flourish; the splendid crowd were in a position to enjoy these hits with a detached aestheticism, and they did. Bradman did not take the field because of a touch of influenza, and McCabe, the acting captain, soon performed with Sievers the ritual of the new ball, then called up O'Reilly and Fleetwood-Smith. As soon as Fleetwood-Smith's hair got into the right position I thought for a moment that Hitler had turned his attention to cricket; he would be a left-hand googly bowler, when you come to think of it.

O'Reilly sent a troublesome over to Barnett, who was twice given out leg-before-wicket unanimously by the crowd; Barnett also lobbed a ball perilously near silly mid-on, and tried to hit Fleetwood-Smith out of sight, but missed his aim easily while Oldfield took the ball wide to leg. The first ball of O'Reilly's next over, a savage top-spinner, defeated Barnett, who, altogether too late, was leg-before, this time without much doubt.

The arrival of Hammond provoked a reception generous and loud. Fleetwood-Smith bowled a good length here-about, and Hammond had to play terribly late to edge a leg-break for four. The Australian attack was at this point extraordinarily good on the true turf, the best we had so far seen in the rubber. And the fielding was keen and on its toes; this was a winning side; it must be nice to know that you have 600 runs and more behind you, as well as forty or fifty thousand people.

Fleetwood-Smith's field included a cover, an extra cover, and a fine mid-off; this cordon stopped a succession of drives by Hammond, classic as the Elgin marbles, but at last Hammond penetrated with a hit of ease and velocity. There is no doubt who is the most *beautiful* batsman in the world.

Worthington plodded honestly, not the savage hooker

and driver who once scandalized the Sheffield crowd by routing Yorkshire before lunch; this was a Worthington of specific gravity. But nearly all contemporary batsmen wear a look of the toiling commonplace when seen in the company of Hammond.

Worthington expired at 65, to a lively leg-spinner by Ward; the Australian bowling was really fine. When Ward turned a ball skilfully, there was the usual talk of spots on the wicket; and of course no wicket on a fifth day can very well be without a blemish, but this wicket was nearly perfect; the bowler seldom is given credit for his art. Hammond banged a full toss from Fleetwood-Smith for four to square leg; none the less Fleetwood-Smith sent along many dexterous spinners, and cast a shadow before him.

After tea, a straight drive by Hammond shot to the boundary with a speed that frustrated the eyesight; the way he pounced on the ball was a wonder of swift, sure energy concealed by beauty. Hammond then reached his 50; the innings was an education in balanced skill, effortless as Kreisler playing the violin, and ripe as the summer of Hammond's career, now at its height.

Suddenly, a great roar announced that Sievers had bowled Hammond with a magnificent ball of crashing pace from the earth.

The match was over, all but the academic details.

---

## SIXTH DAY

### AUSTRALIA First Innings

| | | | | |
|---|---|---|---|---|
| J. H. Fingleton, c. Sims, b. Robins | . | . | . | 38 |
| W. A. Brown, c. Ames, b. Voce | . | . | . | 1 |
| D. G. Bradman, c. Robins, b. Verity | . | . | . | 13 |
| K. E. Rigg, c. Verity, b. Allen | . | . | . | 16 |
| S. J. McCabe, c. Worthington, b. Voce | . | . | 63 |
| L. S. Darling, c. Allen, b. Verity | . | . | . | 20 |

### AUSTRALIA First Innings—*continued*

| | |
|---|---:|
| M. Sievers, st. Ames, b. Robins . . . . | 1 |
| W. A. Oldfield, not out . . . . | 27 |
| W. J. O'Reilly, c. Sims, b. Hammond . | 4 |
| F. Ward, st. Ames, b. Hammond . . . | 7 |
| Extra (b. 2, l.b. 6, n.b. 2) . . . . | 10 |

Total (for 9 wickets) . . . . 200

Innings declared closed.

#### Australia first-innings bowling analysis

| | O. | M. | R. | W. |
|---|---|---|---|---|
| Voce . . . | 18 | 3 | 49 | 2 |
| Allen . . | 12 | 2 | 35 | 1 |
| Sims . . . | 9 | 1 | 35 | 0 |
| Verity . . . | 14 | 4 | 24 | 2 |
| Robins . . . | 7 | 0 | 31 | 2 |
| Hammond . . | 5·3 | 0 | 16 | 2 |

#### Fall of the wickets:

| 1 | 2 | 3 | 4 | 5 | 6 | 7 | 8 | 9 |
|---|---|---|---|---|---|---|---|---|
| 7 | 33 | 69 | 79 | 122 | 130 | 183 | 190 | 200 |

### ENGLAND First Innings

| | |
|---|---:|
| Worthington, c. Bradman, b. McCabe . . | 0 |
| Barnett, c. Darling, b. Sievers . . . . | 11 |
| Hammond, c. Darling, b. Sievers . . . | 32 |
| Leyland, c. Darling, b. O'Reilly . . . | 17 |
| Sims, c. Brown, b. Sievers . . . | 3 |
| Ames, b. Sievers . . . . . . | 3 |
| R. W. V. Robins, c. O'Reilly, b. Sievers . . | 0 |
| Hardstaff, b. O'Reilly . . . . | 3 |
| G. O. Allen, not out . . . . . | 0 |
| Verity, c. Brown, b. O'Reilly . . . . | 0 |
| Extras (b. 5, l.b. 1, n.b. 1) . . . . | 7 |

Total (for 9 wickets) . . . 76

Innings declared closed.

#### England first-innings bowling analysis

| | O. | M. | R. | W. |
|---|---|---|---|---|
| McCabe . . | 2 | 1 | 7 | 1 |
| Sievers . . . | 11·2 | 5 | 21 | 5 |
| O'Reilly . . | 12 | 5 | 28 | 3 |
| Fleetwood-Smith . | 3 | 1 | 13 | 0 |

Fall of the wickets:

| 1 | 2 | 3 | 4 | 5 | 6 | 7 | 8 | 9 |
|---|---|---|---|---|---|---|---|---|
| 0 | 14 | 56 | 68 | 71 | 71 | 67 | 76 | 76 |

## AUSTRALIA SECOND INNINGS

| | |
|---|---|
| W. J. O'Reilly, c. and b. Voce . . . . | 0 |
| L. O'B. Fleetwood-Smith, c. Verity, b. Voce . | 0 |
| F. Ward, c. Hardstaff, b. Verity . . . | 18 |
| K. E. Rigg, l.b.w. (n.), b. Sims . . . . | 47 |
| W. A. Brown, c. Barnett, b. Voce . . . | 20 |
| J. H. Fingleton, c. Ames, b. Sims . . . | 136 |
| D. G. Bradman, c. Allen, b. Verity . . . | 270 |
| S. J. McCabe, l.b.w. (n.), b. Allen . . . | 22 |
| L. S. Darling, b. Allen . . . . . | 0 |
| W. A. Oldfield, l.b.w., b. Verity . . . | 7 |
| M. Sievers, not out . . . . . . | 25 |
| Extras (b. 6, l.b. 2, n.b. 10, w. 1) . . | 19 |
| Total . . . . . . | 564 |

Australia second-innings bowling analysis

| | O. | M. | R. | W. |
|---|---|---|---|---|
| Voce . | 29 | 2 | 120 | 3 |
| Hammond . . | 22 | 3 | 89 | 0 |
| Allen . . . | 23 | 2 | 84 | 2 |
| Verity . . . | 37·7 | 9 | 79 | 3 |
| Robins . . . | 11 | 2 | 46 | 0 |
| Sims . . . | 23 | 1 | 109 | 2 |
| Worthington . . | 4 | 0 | 18 | 0 |

Fall of the wickets:

| 1 | 2 | 3 | 4 | 5 | 6 | 7 | 8 | 9 | 10 |
|---|---|---|---|---|---|---|---|---|---|
| 0 | 3 | 38 | 74 | 97 | 443 | 511 | 511 | 549 | 564 |

## ENGLAND SECOND INNINGS

| | |
|---|---|
| Worthington, c. Sievers, b. Ward . . . | 16 |
| Barnett, l.b.w., b. O'Reilly . . . . | 23 |
| Hammond, b. Sievers . . . . . | 51 |
| Leyland, not out . . . . . | 111 |
| Ames, b. Fleetwood-Smith . . . . | 19 |
| Hardstaff, c. Ward, b. Fleetwood-Smith . | 17 |
| G. O. Allen, c. Sievers, b. Fleetwood-Smith . | 11 |
| R. W. V. Robins, b. O'Reilly . . . . | 61 |

ENGLAND Second Innings—*continued*

Verity, c. McCabe, b. O'Reilly . . . . 11
Sims, l.b.w. (n.), b. Fleetwood-Smith . . . 0
Voce, c. Bradman, b. Fleetwood-Smith . . 0
      Extras . . . . . . . 3

      Total . . . . . . . 323

England second-innings bowling analysis

|  | O. | M. | R. | W. |
|---|---|---|---|---|
| Sievers . . . | 12 | 2 | 39 | 1 |
| McCabe . . | 8 | 0 | 32 | 0 |
| O'Reilly . . | 21 | 6 | 65 | 3 |
| Fleetwood-Smith . | 25·6 | 2 | 124 | 5 |
| Ward . . . | 12 | 1 | 60 | 1 |

Fall of the wickets:

| 1 | 2 | 3 | 4 | 5 | 6 | 7 | 8 | 9 | 10 |
|---|---|---|---|---|---|---|---|---|---|
| 29 | 65 | 117 | 155 | 179 | 195 | 306 | 322 | 323 | 323 |

England died with spirit, after all, thanks to a stand by Leyland and Robins, who for a while treated the Australian attack with open contempt, and set an example which it would have done some of the England batsmen well to follow at Adelaide. The crowd on this last sultry morning was small and quiet, reminding me of a county match at Lord's, which God preserve; for the farther away from it I travel the more I love it.

This sentimental flavour of Lord's received encouragement from the sight of Robins at the wicket, who ran out of his ground nimbly, and drove McCabe for four. His gay, impudent dartings up and down were like a sort of whimsical dance of death in England's extreme hour. Leyland, too, escaped from the entanglements of doubt which for so long had been hindering the free play of his bat. After all, Emmott Robinson's Yorkshire pads are too wide and heavy for anybody else except the original who used them with such obstinacy and foresight. A lusty straight drive by

Leyland knocked the umpire off his balance, and people laughed, as they always laugh when an umpire is hit. The cricket was the most attractive of the match.

Robins reached 50 in forty-seven minutes, and communicated to all of us his enjoyment of his play. He drove O'Reilly through the covers with a lovely forward sweep, and in the same over Leyland hurled his bat straight down the line, and the boundary was struck mightily. This was a good end for England. There was no recklessness in the batting; it observed moderation in excess. An off-drive by Robins from Fleetwood-Smith was a model of style—head down, and body over the ball.

Leyland reached his 100 with two fours, in an eccentric over of Fleetwood-Smith. The second part of the innings was the Yorkshire Leyland, strong in the forearm, and rich of nature and the right accent. At 306 Robins played forward, and over, a ball from O'Reilly and was bowled. O'Reilly had scarcely looked capable of taking a wicket.

The generous Melbourne crowd gave Robins a hearty welcome back to the pavilion, and Verity drove his first ball for four, another injustice to O'Reilly, which was followed by yet another, when Verity glanced a fast ball for four with elegance, and some disdain. Verity was skilfully caught at deep mid-on by McCabe, who picked another libertinous hit from O'Reilly off the ground. Verity's innings was as though Mr. Turveydrop had been observed a little the worse for liquor. The match was over shortly after one o'clock; and I walked back to Melbourne through the lovely gardens which begin a minute or two's walk from the ground. The hot sunshine beat on the grass and flashed on the water-sprays. The tropical foliage hung heavily. Children played under the shady trees. All was happy and restful; Australia were winning the rubber.

# CHAPTER XII

## ADELAIDE AND THE
## OPPORTUNITY

ENGLAND were given another chance at Adelaide, where, on
a beautiful wicket, Australia collapsed after winning the
toss. At close of play on the second afternoon, England had
scored 174 for two, against Australia's 288 all out. The
match was thrown away by a mistaken policy—the 'stay
there and let the the runs come' delusion. But I will tell the
tale of this match as I saw it over by over and as I noted it
down in all the uncertainty of the events as they occurred.
One point only will I emphasize in advance, for the purpose
of giving the key to the issue. The new leg-before-wicket
rule played into Fleetwood-Smith's hands. He is a bowler
who cunningly rings the changes on an off-break and on
his running-away ball, both bowled with much the same
turn of the arm and wrist. The new rule prevented the
English batsmen from putting the pads in front during
their moments of speculation and mental darkness. On the
closing morning England's chance was excellent, though
much depended on Hammond; he was not out 39, and England, three wickets down, wanted 244. With his third ball
Fleetwood-Smith bowled Hammond, all the way; Hammond reached forward, and the ball came back severely and
rapidly. Under the old leg-before-wicket law, Hammond
would have gone back and trusted to his pads as soon as he
realized he was guessing after the first few yards of the
flight; as it was, he was compelled to use his bat—and it
was not wide enough to cover both the break-away for

which he played, and the break that actually happened. The slow-footed methods of post-war English batsmen provided Fleetwood-Smith with easy game on a wicket 'made for him', as they say. Yet to his credit, it must be recorded that he was always beating the bat even on the second day —that is, before the wicket became dusty. A man in the crowd, a Yorkshireman by birth, stated sadly: 'That's where Wally Hammond isn't Don Bradman. They wouldn't have got Don out third ball to-day if Australia had wanted only 244.' The match was thrown away—and England never looked up again. What a fall! Two victories in hand, Hammond at the top of his form, four consecutive hundreds, and then a double hundred at Sydney—yet he was at last put down, suppressed, and the whole of the team with him. It was all strange and disillusioning.

# CHAPTER XIII

# FOURTH TEST—ADELAIDE

*January 29–February 4, 1937*

## FIRST DAY

### AUSTRALIA First Innings

| | |
|---|---:|
| J. H. Fingleton, run out . . . . . | 10 |
| W. A. Brown, c. Allen, b. Farnes . . . | 42 |
| K. E. Rigg, c. Ames, b. Farnes . . . . | 20 |
| D. G. Bradman, b. Allen . . . . . | 26 |
| S. J. McCabe, c. Allen, b. Robins . . . | 88 |
| R. Gregory, l.b.w., b. Hammond . . . | 23 |
| A. G. Chipperfield, not out . . . . | 45 |
| W. A. Oldfield, run out . . . . . | 5 |
| W. J. O'Reilly, not out . . . . . | 3 |
| Extras (l.b. 2, n.b. 3) . . . . . | 5 |

Total (for 7 wickets) . . . . 267

To bat.—E. L. McCormick and L. O'B. Fleetwood-Smith.

### Australia first-innings bowling analysis to date

| | O. | M. | R. | W. |
|---|---|---|---|---|
| Voce . . . | 12 | 0 | 49 | 0 |
| Allen . . . | 13 | 0 | 56 | 1 |
| Farnes . . . | 17 | 1 | 59 | 2 |
| Hammond . . . | 5 | 0 | 25 | 1 |
| Verity . . . | 16 | 4 | 47 | 0 |
| Robins . . . | 7 | 1 | 26 | 1 |

### Fall of the wickets:

| 1 | 2 | 3 | 4 | 5 | 6 | 7 |
|---|---|---|---|---|---|---|
| 26 | 72 | 73 | 136 | 206 | 226 | 249 |

THIS was a day of events hard to explain. On a perfect wicket, Australia's batsmen got themselves out one after another; when the fifth wicket fell, Rigg was the only one who had been technically accounted for. Poor strokes accounted for most of his colleagues. Before lunch, I was resigned to a vast Australian total; during ninety minutes the England attack seemed harmless, and in that period the only wicket taken was run out. I thought at this point that bowling for run-outs would be the wisest plan England could put into force. Then Farnes changed the course and temper of everything in eight balls. Bradman was a ghost of his true self again, and but for a pedigree innings by McCabe, Australia would have been in Queer Street. As my narrative will show, Allen's lucky star shone—for the last time. He baffled some of us after tea by keeping Robins on and not claiming the new ball at once. Robins threatened to throw fours away prodigiously, and McCabe punished him severely; yet Robins took McCabe's wicket at the pinch, with a long-hop of aimless direction.

McCabe's innings was pure batsmanship. At his best he is the aristocrat of his side. Chipperfield played another plucky innings, when his side's ship seemed ready to founder with all hands. England's team work was capital. They deserved their day out.

Here was the Australian summer day I have dreamed about on many a cold winter night in England. The Adelaide Oval was almost self-consciously lovely under a sky of delicate blue with flakes of light cloud, like veins in some porcelain dome through which the radiant light of the sun shone and warmed the world. The heat shimmered on the distant hills, and the steeples of the cathedral were given the clear outline of an old-time stage setting. Nature in Australia confirms the school of the nineteenth-century scene-painters; Hawes Craven was entirely true to life. The productions at Daly's held up the mirror faithfully.

The players took the field like lambs to the slaughter, and

the batsmen, having eaten a more or less hearty breakfast, walked unsupported to the wicket. England chose Farnes instead of Sims—fast bowling again being England's spearhead on the ground which, when I was a little boy, was called the fast bowler's graveyard. One or two overs by Voce and Allen told us the pitch was flawless, and deepened the dreams of rich runs to come.

At the risk of breaking his spinal column, Allen caused a ball to rise wrist high, but Fingleton could play back to it at leisure. Voce in vain heaved into play all of his brawn; in quick time his bowling became black in the face, and in twenty minutes Farnes came on, and Voce changed ends. The batsmen were busy dispersing flies; they were at liberty almost to catch them while the ball was coming off the ground. When Farnes actually compelled Fingleton to hurry to get his bat away from an out-swinger, this was a remarkable piece of rhythmical propulsion. On this turf, I felt, a batsman would get out only by absence of mind or by that deep-seated periodic law of human frailty which causes even Heifetz to play a wrong note.

The first wicket fell as a flat consequence of unreason. Several times Fingleton and Brown ran runs which seemed rather agitated, and after a narrow escape and some overthrows, Brown changed his mind, and Fingleton was fatally suspended, so to say, in a physical and mental midair.

Farnes attacked accurately; one ball from him committed the scandal of keeping low, and Brown examined the earth incredulously and seemed at a loss for words. The batting was, of course, slow, as on principle it must be in a Test match upon which hangs an awful Empire-shaking issue. Brown drove Hammond straight; he seemed at ease. An occasional difficulty for the batsmen just now was nothing worse than the pea which was hidden under the soft cushioned bed of the Princess in the fairy tale.

Towards one o'clock Verity came on, set his field to a fraction of an inch, and no doubt the broadcasting people announced that he was about to bowl a maiden—and he did. His loose, boneless action, and his curving length, lulled our senses. Verity is a patient student in quest of the absolute; he seems to bowl in a vacuum, for the quality of his art is not related to finite and vulgar things such as boundaries or wickets. Here is bowling for bowling's sake, seen under the conditions of eternity.

At the other end, Allen suddenly unleashed a kicker which nearly knocked Rigg over—a ball of rare temper, a sort of oath of impatience and frustration. The game called for some exercise of will power; the circumstances governing it were static. We watched the beginning of a war of attrition; this was only the first digging of the trenches, the laying of the sapper's secret mine. Then, after lunch, without giving us due warning, the game entered the regions of the fantastic. Farnes took two wickets in one over, so unlikely a deed, so miraculous, that I could not believe my spectacles. Few of us thought Australia would lose more than three wickets all day. Farnes worked up pace, and from his upright position swung down a fine length. Brown vaguely held out his bat and fell to an easy catch at fine short-leg. Rigg snicked to Ames a ball vivid in velocity, which bounced more than the stumps' height. It was bowling vehement in spirit and stylish in technique.

Farnes forced both Bradman and McCabe back. The match had suffered a change—from slow fires of peace preparing for war to red-hot war at grips. The sapper had been sapped, his own mining operations had been mined.

Bradman and McCabe needed all their experience and

skill to hold back the advancing, and probably rather astonished, England team; each batsman resisted admirably with defence and offence mingled proportionately. McCabe lent his own flexible wrists to his strokes, and though Bradman was more or less passive—he batted nearly an hour for 20 —he had a secure and collected look. But when Bradman was 16 and Australia 109 for three, a dazzling ball from Allen flashed past his bat's edge, and there was a loud but unavailing appeal for a catch at the wicket. It seemed a perilously near thing; Ames's catch was magnificent, and Allen swallowed emotion at the umpire's decision.

The cricket was hereabout beautifully forked with the lightning of antagonism. You could feel currents of electricity in the air; another wicket taken or lost now would signify much, perhaps everything, in the struggle's end. And at twenty-five past three Bradman was bowled by Allen, woefully bowled. He tried a pull, and his bat swung unbeautifully—Don's great shots often offend style when they do not come off. When Allen saw the stumps behind Bradman knocked awry he did not smile, he merely turned his back on the ruin and walked grimly again to his bowling place. Probably he could not believe in a Bradman who remained at the wickets sixty-five minutes and hit no fours. I couldn't, and again I trembled.

Crisis simmered when young Gregory came in, and it was charming to see the seasoned McCabe greeting him with words of encouragement and advice. At once Gregory made the strokes of a natural cricketer; a leg hit off Verity possessed quickness and excellent balance. All the same, Verity's variations worried the boy.

A great pull by McCabe off Farnes was one of the thrilling strokes of the match. He was at his very best, quick to punish, yet always watchful. After tea he hit Robins for ten

in one over, and pulled Voce for four, by strokes as effortless as a man trying a bat's swing in a shop. There is no
cricketer I would rather watch than McCabe in form: he
scores with a courtliness that even the toiling bowlers must
appreciate: he is never brutal, never a plunderer of runs
with a bludgeon, but a sort of Claude Duval of the crease,
taking his booty with gallantry.

Gregory played his part in an important stand. The cool-
ness of Australia's young men throughout the rubber was
in strong contrast to the dithers exhibited by one or two of
England's hardened professionals. Gregory has an old head
on his shoulders, and English cricket-fields will shortly see
him and welcome him into the company of Australia's most
gifted players. He uses his feet, and no doubt time and
experience will strengthen his hits to the offside.

Allen did not claim the new ball at 200; daringly he
trusted to Robins, who, most balls, threatened a two-
bouncer. Allen's luck laughed or grimaced yet again when
McCabe pulled a long hop to his hands at mid-on. One after
another, as I say, Australia's batsmen got themselves out.
Gregory succumbed to Hammond; another victory for
Allen, who, contrary to expectations, gave the new ball to
Hammond, not to Voce or himself. England's attack
thrived on weakness. Considering the beauty of the Adelaide pitch it was a revolt in heaven; the fast bowling,
especially Farnes, conquered the turf with a spirit and skill
which the crowd appreciated generously. A swift throw-in
overwhelmed Oldfield. England's fielding all day was correct and hostile. I could not account for so much irresolute
batsmanship on a wicket calculated to break the heart of any
bowler who ever lived. The rubber was once more placed
in England's lap; fortune almost implored us on bended
knees to take it.

## SECOND DAY

### AUSTRALIA First Innings

| | |
|---|---:|
| J. H. Fingleton, run out . . . . . | 10 |
| W. A. Brown, c. Allen, b. Farnes . . . | 42 |
| K. E. Rigg, c. Ames, b. Farnes . . . . | 20 |
| D. G. Bradman, b. Allen . . . . | 26 |
| S. J. McCabe, c. Allen, b. Robins . . . | 88 |
| R. Gregory, l.b.w., b. Hammond . . . | 23 |
| A. G. Chipperfield, not out . . . . | 57 |
| W. A. Oldfield, run out . . . . . | 5 |
| W. J. O'Reilly, c. Leyland, b. Allen . . . | 7 |
| E. L. McCormick, c. Ames, b. Hammond . . | 4 |
| L. O'B. Fleetwood-Smith, b. Farnes . . . | 1 |
| Extras (l.b. 2, n.b. 3) . . . . . | 5 |
| Total . . . . . . | 288 |

### Australia first-innings bowling analysis

| | O. | M. | R. | W. |
|---|---:|---:|---:|---:|
| Voce . . . | 12 | 0 | 49 | 0 |
| Allen . . . | 16 | 0 | 60 | 2 |
| Farnes . . . | 20·6 | 1 | 71 | 3 |
| Hammond . . | 6 | 0 | 30 | 2 |
| Verity . . . | 16 | 4 | 47 | 0 |
| Robins . . . | 7 | 1 | 26 | 1 |

### Fall of the wickets:

| 1 | 2 | 3 | 4 | 5 | 6 | 7 | 8 | 9 | 10 |
|---|---|---|---|---|---|---|---|---|---|
| 26 | 72 | 73 | 136 | 206 | 226 | 249 | 271 | 283 | 288 |

### ENGLAND First Innings

| | |
|---|---:|
| Barnett, not out . . . . | 92 |
| Verity, c. Bradman, b. O'Reilly . . . | 19 |
| Hammond, c. McCormick, b. O'Reilly . . | 20 |
| Leyland, not out . . . . . | 35 |
| Extras (b. 3, n.b. 4, w. 1) . . . | 8 |
| Total (for 2 wickets) . . . | 174 |

To bat.—G. O. Allen, R. W. V. Robins, R. E. S. Wyatt, K. Farnes, Ames, Hardstaff, Voce.

England first-innings bowling analysis to date

|  | O. | M. | R. | W. |
|---|---|---|---|---|
| McCormick . . | 12 | 1 | 39 | 0 |
| McCabe . . | 7 | 2 | 13 | 0 |
| Fleetwood-Smith . | 21 | 4 | 65 | 0 |
| O'Reilly . . | 14 | 5 | 18 | 2 |
| Chipperfield . . | 6 | 1 | 17 | 0 |
| Gregory . . | 3 | 0 | 14 | 0 |

Fall of the wickets:

| 1 | 2 |
|---|---|
| 53 | 108 |

England's batting did not tell us of a triumphant spirit, but rather of a distrust in the slippery slopes leading to victory. On a wicket fit for a batsman's heaven England seemed to play simply to stay at the wicket, leaving runs to come as a sort of by-product of defensive strokes. In one hundred and seventy minutes only 100 runs were scored. The Australian attack was steady, and Fleetwood-Smith at times bowled a wonderful spinner, but Verity's ability to bat for more than an hour and a half spoke a significant tale.

Hammond was nearly strokeless, and he fell to an error of judgment; he glanced to leg and was caught, for all the world as though he had forgotten the fielder's presence. It often happens at cricket that deliberate slowness leads batsmen to some sudden aberration of the intellect. Barnett was austere, too, and he enjoyed fortune against Fleetwood-Smith.

The game at the end of the second day was anybody's, and anybody might have had it as far as I was concerned. So far it had been sadly short of style; McCabe had played the one and only innings of relish and art. Less than 200 runs in a day, with the best bowler tamed by the modern groundsman's fell arts—this was Lancashire and Yorkshire, without the funny bits.

The morning was warm; as I entered the ground I felt the flavour of a greenhouse. The Englishman cannot help thinking of St. James's Park as he walks to this sumptuous cricket-field through the gardens with the lake, and along the broad avenue which might easily be adorned by Carlton House Terrace. The tropical palms and the plenteous sunshine tell the Englishman where really he is; a flood of light was over the Adelaide Oval's grass, and before the match went forward again a waltz by Waldteufel was broadcast to the waiting crowd, an old strain from Vienna, which seemed to go into the beauty of the scene and the morning. There was something moving about it all. My mind flashed to England, hidden in the winter's cold fogs. Soon the morning papers there would be seized by the crowds going to work, and they would be sending out to us their wishes, hopes, and apprehensions.

O'Reilly came out with Chipperfield in the position of an opening batsman for Australia; the innings was beginning once more, so to say, with much lost ground to be won back. O'Reilly took guard watchfully, then surveyed the English field, no doubt making a mental note of the quickest and shortest cuts to the fence. He played majestically, almost upright, his nose disdaining the ball. He scored one or two runs heedless of consequences before giving a pretty little catch to close mid-on. The pitch was rather faster than it was on the first day, and O'Reilly no doubt consoled himself as he departed by thinking that he would shortly be given another and lengthier opportunity of looking at it. Allen and Farnes attacked; Voce was absent, troubled with some pain in his back. I felt I must, on behalf of the overworked Press, dislocate or fracture an adjective.

Amid loud applause, Chipperfield reached a plucky and gallant 50. He had the honour of carrying out his bat when

Fleetwood-Smith, looking more like Hitler than ever, heard his off stump ejected by Farnes with a most Nazi violence. Thus Australia failed to score 300; I should have thought that rare skill was needed to get out for less than 600 on such a paradise of a wicket.

At five minutes to one Verity went in first for England with Barnett, and so followed the example of the incomparable Wilfred Rhodes, who also began cricket as a slow left-handed bowler, and vowed when young that he would open an England innings and score a century against Australia, which he did. Verity wore the disguise of a cap, and McCormick appeared intent on removing it. One ball in his preliminary over rose to a height never achieved, if attempted, by England's fast bowlers.

Barnett cracked McCormick for four from the back foot, and the speed of the hit reduced cover-point temporarily to the immobility of a caryatid. McCormick proceeded next to endanger Barnett's skull and thinking parts; he was very fast—so much so that one ball buried itself in Oldfield's gloves before Verity had concluded his stroke. McCormick next chipped the edge of Verity's bat, and a new weapon was called for. All these quaint occurrences reminded me of the story J. T. Tyldesley once told me of the first time he met Kortright of Essex. 'I played forward, and the next thing I remembered was Russell, the wicket-keeper, saying, "It's all right, Johnny, here's your bat".' For about six overs McCormick is one of the fastest bowlers of modern times.

Fleetwood-Smith bowled five minutes before lunch, and Verity helped himself to three off a long-hop, but Fleetwood-Smith beat Barnett with a glorious spinner from leg to an inch or so past the off stump, as clever and artistic a ball as any seen so far in the rubber. England avoided

major disasters in that trying half-hour which always pre-
cedes an interval, and I left with relief the humid shade of
the Press box, searching eagerly for refreshment.

Barnett after lunch pulled McCormick imperially for
four, and then played rather helplessly at a potential kicker
from McCormick, who could not hold the return catch as
he reeled down the pitch following through. McCormick
obtained rare pace out of the ground, but his tearaway
action did not spell class or endurance. Fleetwood-Smith
was the incalculable artist; he bowled another accurate over,
then sent a full toss, which Barnett pulled for six with con-
temptuous ease. Meanwhile Verity declined to get out as
quickly as he was expected to; he played back scornfully and
retained his cap. It is, perhaps, as well that cricket is not
played by the book of arithmetic (in Mercutio's phrase);
if it were we should now have had before us a pretty problem. If Verity was capable of staying in against a fresh and
hopeful Australian attack, how long would it take to get
Hammond out later during the proceedings? The joy of the
game is that even a Hammond is not armed against the
possibility of a duck first ball to a full toss.

The Australian bowling was not at this point consistently dangerous; Fleetwood-Smith, of course, has a licence
for experiments. If I were his captain I should fine him for
every maiden over he bowled. But O'Reilly dropped too
canny a length; and McCormick was all over the place,
though bracingly fast and enthusiastic; he aimed right and
left of the target, too often out of the bat's danger-zone.
Still, England could not get on with the game. In one hundred minutes only 53 were made. Verity is not a stroke
player; he bats, as he bowls, in the academic abstract. He
was caught finely at deep leg as a consequence of a display
of human vanity. Nor was Barnett yet at his best; he mis-

timed several swings to leg from long-hops by Fleetwood-Smith, and seemed willing to get to the other end of the wicket, where, no doubt, spin becomes an object of pure aesthetic contemplation. And all the time the afternoon became hotter, and I surveyed the line of the hills and envied their peacefulness.

A stroke by Hammond to the off as soon as he came in disturbed these drowsy reflections; he pushed out at O'Reilly and nearly sent a catch. England's innings had not yet emerged from the vague and indecisive, and Hammond was out for all he knew when he played forward at Fleetwood-Smith, and the ball somehow skimmed to Chipperfield, who missed a chance at slip. The Australian attack improved considerably; I thought to myself, if so much spin can be employed on the wicket now, then heaven help England in the fourth innings. Fleetwood-Smith was excellent and original, and O'Reilly always a model of perspiring persistence. Hammond attempted no strokes, and his advent at the crease produced depression.

After tea, Fleetwood-Smith again beat Barnett with a masterpiece of curving flight and biting spin; this bowler's craft on the flawless ground was often a joy to watch, and it told of more genius than anything that a batsman could show us in circumstances which should have bred runs profusely. The bowler, as I have twice said before, gets little recognition; everybody can discern the merit of a hit to the boundary, but only a few the subtle work of fingers and wrist. Given an honest share of luck, Fleetwood-Smith might have taken three wickets or four by the time England's total reached 100. Considering the amount of spin he exploited, his control was capital.

Barnett's 50 arrived after a period of severe discipline for him, the cricketer who in his natural mood is one of the finest stroke-players in the game. I suppose it was all for the cause: in Test cricket we scorn delights and live laborious days. Barnett's service to England was beyond estimation. At twenty minutes to five Hammond lost his wicket, to his unconcealed chagrin. He glanced O'Reilly to leg, where McCormick held a baby's catch. Leyland put new spirit into the batting. None the less the pace of scoring was not good enough for a side that wishes to win at Adelaide against the handicap of a fourth innings. Fleetwood-Smith and O'Reilly always called for close inspection, but McCabe, with an old ball, and Chipperfield, might have been hit, and would have been hit by Barnett in a Gloucestershire match. A bad ball is a bad ball whether bowled by myself, Arthur Mailey, Sidney Barnes, or by Charles Fry in the middle of a sentence.

---

## THIRD DAY

### AUSTRALIA First Innings

| | |
|---|---:|
| J. H. Fingleton, run out | 10 |
| W. A. Brown, c. Allen, b. Farnes | 42 |
| K. E. Rigg, c. Ames, b. Farnes | 20 |
| D. G. Bradman, b. Allen | 26 |
| S. J. McCabe, c. Allen, b. Robins | 88 |
| R. Gregory, l.b.w., b. Hammond | 23 |
| A. G. Chipperfield, not out | 57 |
| W. A. Oldfield, run out | 5 |
| W. J. O'Reilly, c. Leyland, b. Allen | 7 |
| E. L. McCormick, c. Ames, b. Hammond | 4 |
| L. O'B. Fleetwood-Smith, b. Farnes | 1 |
| Extras (l.b., 2, n.b. 3) | 5 |
| Total | 288 |

### Australia first-innings bowling analysis

| | O. | M. | R. | W. |
|---|---:|---:|---:|---:|
| Voce | 12 | 0 | 49 | 0 |
| Allen | 16 | 0 | 60 | 2 |
| Farnes | 20·6 | 1 | 71 | 3 |
| Hammond | 6 | 0 | 30 | 2 |
| Verity | 16 | 4 | 47 | 0 |
| Robins | 7 | 1 | 26 | 1 |

## Fall of the wickets:

| 1 | 2 | 3 | 4 | 5 | 6 | 7 | 8 | 9 | 10 |
|---|---|---|---|---|---|---|---|---|---|
| 26 | 72 | 73 | 136 | 206 | 226 | 249 | 271 | 283 | 288 |

### ENGLAND First Innings

| | |
|---|---:|
| Barnett, l.b.w., b. Fleetwood-Smith . . . | 129 |
| Verity, c. Bradman, b. O'Reilly . . . . | 19 |
| Hammond, c. McCormick, b. O'Reilly . . | 20 |
| Leyland, c. Chipperfield, b. Fleetwood-Smith . | 45 |
| R. E. S. Wyatt, c. Fingleton, b. O'Reilly . . | 3 |
| Ames, b. McCormick . . . . . | 52 |
| Hardstaff, c. and b. McCormick . . . . | 20 |
| G. O. Allen, l.b.w., b. Fleetwood-Smith . . | 11 |
| R. W. V. Robins, c. Oldfield, b. O'Reilly . . | 10 |
| Voce, c. Rigg, b. Fleetwood-Smith . . . | 8 |
| K. Farnes, not out . . . . . . | 0 |
| Extras (b. 6, l.b. 2, n.b. 4, w. 1) . . . | 13 |
| Total . . . . . . | 330 |

### England first-innings bowling analysis

| | O. | M. | R. | W. |
|---|---|---|---|---|
| McCormick . . | 21 | 2 | 81 | 2 |
| McCabe . . | 9 | 2 | 18 | 0 |
| Fleetwood-Smith . | 41·4 | 10 | 129 | 4 |
| O'Reilly . . | 30 | 12 | 51 | 4 |
| Chipperfield . . | 9 | 1 | 24 | 0 |
| Gregory . . | 3 | 0 | 14 | 0 |

## Fall of the wickets:

| 1 | 2 | 3 | 4 | 5 | 6 | 7 | 8 | 9 | 10 |
|---|---|---|---|---|---|---|---|---|---|
| 53 | 108 | 190 | 195 | 259 | 299 | 304 | 318 | 322 | 330 |

### AUSTRALIA Second Innings

| | |
|---|---:|
| J. H. Fingleton, l.b.w., b. Hammond . . . | 12 |
| W. A. Brown, not out . . . . . | 23 |
| D. G. Bradman, not out . . . . . | 26 |
| Extras (b. 1, l.b. 1) . . . . . | 2 |
| Total (for 1 wicket) . . . . | 63 |

Australia second-innings bowling analysis to date

|          | O. | M. | R. | W. |
|----------|----|----|----|----|
| Farnes . . . | 7 | 1 | 20 | 0 |
| Hammond . . | 6 | 0 | 19 | 1 |
| Allen . . . | 4 | 1 | 12 | 0 |
| Voce . . . | 4 | 2 | 8 | 0 |
| Verity . . . | 4 | 2 | 2 | 0 |

Fall of the wicket:

1
—
21

We have enjoyed a ding-dong battle to-day, and though on paper the issue is even, I doubt England's chances in the fourth innings. The wicket is already not unhelpful to spin bowling controlled by the full power of the wrist; it is not yet ready for Verity, who is purely a finger-spin bowler. England's batting did its best against an attack of rare excellence. Fleetwood-Smith's analysis is misleading; it was he who disturbed the English confidence by bowling touched with the incalculable properties of genius. Considering the amount of break he exploited, his length was astonishingly good. England's batsmen throughout the tour did not shape well against slow spin, and the truth is that a vast total was not to be confidently expected from them unless Hammond scored heavily.

Bradman was at his most ominous that evening. So long as he is unbeaten, Australia must always be said to have a firm grip on the proceedings.

The week-end was an oven, and we escaped to the hills, thanks to the hospitality of Adelaide. In the the night I heard the wind in the tall trees outside my bedroom window, and I concluded that once more rain had come to spoil fair sport. But there was no rain, only a refreshing clearance of the air. We returned to Adelaide by car. The day was a public holiday, and we met an endless procession of vehicles leaving the city, all sorts of conveyances—new cars, old cars, charabancs, lorries, shays, drags, bicycles, all packed with people. I thought they were refugees flying from the horrors of the Test match, women and children first. Some of the men had stuck to their posts almost to the end, for they had come away without their coats, even without their waistcoats and watch-chains. When we reached Adelaide it seemed that the evacuation had been successfully carried out; we saw no sign of life for a mile, only a recumbent dog, the last of the garrison. Alas! a vast number of inhabitants had been trapped; the cricket ground was full, a besieged city waiting for deliverance from the English batting.

Again the day was a midsummer welter of sunshine, with a healthy wind in the sky's blue awning, and again the radio's music entertained the waiting crowd. There was a performance on the bones. 'I have a tolerable ear for music', said Bottom the weaver, ' Let's have the tongs and the bones.'

Quickly the game got to grips. Leyland made six from the first over bowled by Fleetwood-Smith, including a superb square cut. Barnett jumped to a half volley from O'Reilly, and when he was 98 O'Reilly tried artfully to get him caught at short leg, but Barnett was wise, though he nearly ran himself out in the same over. Fleetwood-Smith's next over accounted for Leyland with a beautiful spinning-away ball which drew him out and found the bat's edge; Chipperfield's catch was quick and certain, Fleetwood-Smith deserved his wicket, and the score-board scandalously announced his analysis now to be one for 77. He was again turning quickly, and if he wavered in length that was the price he had naturally to pay for his ability to give the batsmen constant reason for thought and delayed strokes.

Barnett reached his hundred at twenty-five minutes past twelve—a long innings for him, but one of magnificent self-denial. He proved that he can lend discipline to his strokes, and put forward a technique governed by judgment.

Wyatt was immediately caught at silly forward short leg, and the crowd woke up and rejoiced. England's advantage had gone; the stone was at the bottom of the hill again; Sisyphus had to begin his labours afresh. Fleetwood-Smith beat Barnett yet another time—a lovely break from leg, sharp as a knife, which caused Barnett to jump as though stung. All of us now knew that in a fourth innings on a dry turf England would suffer severely if they had to make 300. Oh! for the 100 additional runs which surely could have been scored on Saturday against McCabe, Chipperfield, and a worn-out team.

Success transformed the Australians marvellously. The field became a net, the wicket a delusion and a snare. The crowd were hungry for the collapse which threatened England, as Ames joined Barnett looking stern and far away from the fields of Kent and the bunting and the music. The game was at a turning point. I cannot praise with too much warmth the skill of Fleetwood-Smith and O'Reilly on a turf which was the open enemy of any bowling not alive with spin or fundamental brainwork. It was, none the less, a turf obviously conniving an alliance with spin.

A swift back-stroke by Ames to the on boundary off O'Reilly brought some flush of colour back to England's innings. It had turned pallid. Barnett in an hour scored only 13, and after passing his 100 he seemed to bat myopically, especially against Fleetwood-Smith. He found quick eyesight for McCormick, though, when O'Reilly rested, and the new ball was ready. He cut twice for fours, glanced

exquisitely for four, all wrists and poise, snicked for four a
prodigiously fast ball, sending an impossible chance to
deep fine slip. Four boundaries in eight balls—most in-
decorous behaviour in a harrowing Test match. Ames
played well, and when Fleetwood-Smith came back just
before lunch he pulled and drove him savagely for fours.
Ames throughout the season showed skill against spin,
and promised a long innings—a wicket-keeper who for
years has had opportunity to study Freeman on English
wickets should have acquired a sense of the googly.

At lunch the see-saw was achieving the balance of
equality again. And immediately after lunch Australia made
a big advance. Barnett jumped to an almost full-toss,
heaved his bat across the flight, and missed. He was leg-
before, probably on his big toe. Ironical game! Fleetwood-
Smith beat Barnett thrice in vain, with superb spin, and at
last got his wicket by chance. Barnett was never comfortable against the spin, but this fact only stressed the discipline and doggedness of his long, valuable, and brave
innings.

Ames hit O'Reilly for a crashing four past mid-off, a
welcome to Hardstaff, whose great opportunity had now
come with open and appealing hands. Three fieldsmen
crouched at Hardstaff's feet like children listening to a nur-
sery story: 'Once upon a time I was a brilliant batsman at
Trent Bridge.' Hardstaff survived many problematical
moments; his bat was all ambiguous pushes at the spin, but
he looked up as soon as McCormick bowled honest, straight
speed at him. Yet England could not make the headway
they needed, with the threat of a fourth innings always
before them. Ames reached a gallant and cultured 50, and
was bowled soon after in an attempt to swing a quick ball
to leg. It was exasperating that England to-day should be

losing wickets to efforts at strokes in an innings generally dour and protective in outlook. Hardstaff also perished in the process of performing a hook, though he probably was moved purely by reflex action. The ball reared late. McCormick attacked keenly now. What a good sparkling wine comes to a bowler when he gets somebody out. McCormick seems dependent on constant results. Robins began with a curious series of reactions against Fleetwood-Smith. He missed his stroke; he snicked to the boots of slip and also he came near to running himself out. Then Mc-Cormick hit him alarmingly between wind and water. Allen set him the example of reason and responsibility for a few moments, until the captain himself played forward and was leg-before. England were collapsing with regularity. The folk who had fled the Test match could safely and with appetite return. England's calculations on Saturday of a lead of 250 appeared in a pretty light now. Rigg caught Voce coolly from a towering clout to the on. Australia bowled and fielded with all the traditional skill and voracity. O'Reilly nearly achieved the cunning we saw from him a year or two ago in England. But it was Fleetwood-Smith who really disturbed the confidence of the English batsmen.

Hammond bowled one over when Australia's second innings began; Allen went on then with Farnes at the other end. Neither Farnes nor Allen could cause Fingleton or Brown to slice his strokes to the new ball, and Hammond returned. The wicket was not really a fast bowler's; it was fit for spin, controlled not only by finger, but also by the full power of the wrist. I doubted if Verity would be dangerous on it yet. He is entirely a finger-spin bowler. In half an hour Allen tried four bowlers. Clearly he was investigating the pitch, and rather in the dark about it. Hammond took the first wicket—Fingleton, leg before.

Bradman began with the utmost confidence, scoring off nearly every ball sent to him. He and Brown ran quick singles, and hysteria appeared in the crowd in the shape of a woman, or a thousand women. The fight was magnificent. You could feel the physical strain from the edge of the field. The two teams were beautifully matched, even if they were not great teams. In the charming Adelaide Club that night, I and a friend were dined with warmth. The Adelaide Club is always hospitable, but this night there was an additional fervour in the assembly.

## FOURTH DAY

### AUSTRALIA First Innings

| | |
|---|---:|
| J. H. Fingleton, run out | 10 |
| W. A. Brown, c. Allen, b. Farnes | 42 |
| K. E. Rigg, c. Ames, b. Farnes | 20 |
| D. G. Bradman, b. Allen | 26 |
| S. J. McCabe, c. Allen, b. Robins | 88 |
| R. Gregory, l.b.w., b. Hammond | 23 |
| A. G. Chipperfield, not out | 57 |
| W. A. Oldfield, run out | 5 |
| W. J. O'Reilly, c. Leyland, b. Allen | 7 |
| E. L. McCormick, c. Ames, b. Hammond | 4 |
| L. O'B. Fleetwood-Smith, b. Farnes | 1 |
| Extras (l.b. 2, n.b. 3) | 5 |
| Total | 288 |

### Australia first-innings bowling analysis

| | O. | M. | R. | W. |
|---|---:|---:|---:|---:|
| Voce | 12 | 0 | 49 | 0 |
| Allen | 16 | 0 | 60 | 2 |
| Farnes | 20.6 | 1 | 71 | 3 |
| Hammond | 6 | 0 | 30 | 2 |
| Verity | 16 | 4 | 47 | 0 |
| Robins | 7 | 1 | 26 | 1 |

### Fall of the wickets:

| 1 | 2 | 3 | 4 | 5 | 6 | 7 | 8 | 9 | 10 |
|---|---|---|---|---|---|---|---|---|---|
| 26 | 72 | 73 | 136 | 206 | 226 | 249 | 271 | 283 | 288 |

## ENGLAND First Innings

| | |
|---|---:|
| Barnett, l.b.w., b. Fleetwood-Smith . . . | 129 |
| Verity, c. Bradman, b. O'Reilly . . . | 19 |
| Hammond, c. McCormick, b. O'Reilly . . | 20 |
| Leyland, c. Chipperfield, b. Fleetwood-Smith . | 45 |
| R. E. S. Wyatt, c. Fingleton, b. O'Reilly . . | 3 |
| Ames, b. McCormick . . . . | 52 |
| Hardstaff, c. and b. McCormick . . . | 20 |
| G. O. Allen, l.b.w., b. Fleetwood-Smith . . | 11 |
| R. W. V. Robins, c. Oldfield, b. O'Reilly . | 10 |
| Voce, c. Rigg, b. Fleetwood-Smith . . . | 8 |
| K. Farnes, not out . . . . . | 0 |
| Extras (b. 6, l.b. 2, n.b. 4, w. 1) . . . | 13 |
| Total . . . . . . | 330 |

### England first-innings bowling analysis

| | O. | M. | R. | W. |
|---|---|---|---|---|
| McCormick . . | 21 | 2 | 81 | 2 |
| McCabe . . | 9 | 2 | 18 | 0 |
| Fleetwood-Smith . | 41·4 | 10 | 129 | 4 |
| O'Reilly . . | 30 | 12 | 51 | 4 |
| Chipperfield . . | 9 | 1 | 24 | 0 |
| Gregory . . | 3 | 0 | 14 | 0 |

### Fall of the wickets:

| 1 | 2 | 3 | 4 | 5 | 6 | 7 | 8 | 9 | 10 |
|---|---|---|---|---|---|---|---|---|---|
| 53 | 108 | 190 | 195 | 259 | 299 | 304 | 318 | 322 | 330 |

## AUSTRALIA Second Innings

| | |
|---|---:|
| J. H. Fingleton, l.b.w., b. Hammond . . . | 12 |
| W. A. Brown, c. Ames, b. Voce . . . | 32 |
| D. G. Bradman, not out . . . . | 174 |
| S. J. McCabe, c. Wyatt, b. Robins . . . | 55 |
| K. E. Rigg, c. Hammond, b. Farnes . . . | 7 |
| R. Gregory, not out . . . . . | 36 |
| Extras (b. 10, l.b. 13, n.b. 1, w. 1) . . | 25 |
| Total (for 4 wickets) . . . | 341 |

### Australia second-innings bowling analysis to date

| | O. | M. | R. | W. |
|---|---|---|---|---|
| Farnes . . . | 18 | 1 | 69 | 1 |
| Hammond . . . | 11 | 0 | 37 | 1 |
| Allen . . . | 11 | 1 | 44 | 0 |
| Voce . . . | 16 | 2 | 59 | 1 |
| Verity . . . | 32 | 12 | 54 | 0 |
| Robins . . . | 6 | 0 | 38 | 1 |
| Barnett . . . | 5 | 1 | 15 | 0 |

Fall of the wickets:

| 1 | 2 | 3 | 4 |
|---|---|---|---|
| 21 | 88 | 197 | 237 |

A gruelling day ended with the match in Australia's lap.
Short of historic batsmanship in the fourth innings, England would certainly lose, for the wicket would go on
lending aid to O'Reilly and Fleetwood-Smith, unless an
amount of rain came to bind the gently worn places together. And at close of play a comprehensive miracle was
needed to provoke rain from Adelaide's spacious blue sky.

Once more Bradman was Australia's spinal column.
Had he failed, the rubber would on the fourth evening have
been in England's hands. He never fails when he knows
that a rubber depends on him. Bradman served the cause
with an almost moral control of his customary avaricious-
ness. He batted grammatically, committed no vanities.
Only once did he attack, and that was while the English
bowling temporarily lost certainty of touch.

Allen bowled only a few overs because of a strained leg.
England's chief lack was leg-spin. I suggested early in the
match that finger-spin, as distinct from wrist-spin, would
not find out those places on the pitch which Fleetwood-
Smith was seeking on Monday. Verity bowled ably to keep
Bradman quiet this evening, but that was all he could do.

Voce's third ball of the day struck Bradman's pad, and
there was a loud, almost desperate, appeal, which ascended
to the blue heavens and was lost there—the umpire ignored
it, rather than dismissed it. Bradman glanced Farnes
swiftly to leg, yet he had time to spare, so quick was he to
see the ball and, instinctively as a ballet dancer, to move his
feet. And when he played back to Voce his bat was
ominously straight. His genius now moved in the reins of

judgment. Voce's attack could be waited for with a show of patience; neither he nor Farnes was able consistently to obtain from the wicket the disturbing velocity of Mc-Cormick, though one ball from Farnes kept low, and Bradman snicked it perilously to the slips.

I was beginning to see the partnership between Bradman and Brown throwing roots to the earth when another sudden fast one, this time from Voce, was glanced by Brown behind the wicket, inches from the ground to leg, extremely fine, where Ames made a beautiful and un-emotional catch.

Verity came on and endeavoured hard to spin, but in vain; still he worried McCabe twice in quick sequence. Meanwhile Voce, stimulated by a quick wicket as though by champagne, or, as he himself might prefer to say, by four ale, increased his powers, and nearly got McCabe caught at forward mid-on.

The struggle was severe, nobly severe, and a glorious jumping off-drive by Bradman off Verity was retaliatory as much as it was an act of offence. Verity moved Hammond from first slip for McCabe and placed him at silly point a yard from Wyatt, a device which suggested he was expecting the ball to jump slightly rather than to spin. England obviously realized, with every nerve of consciousness, that on the stand by Bradman and McCabe hung the fate of the match, and, maybe, of the rubber. They strove so strenuously that currents of determination shot over the field, and could be felt at the boundary's edge like invisible arrows of pain.

A violent bumper by Farnes was hooked vehemently by Bradman, and in the same over McCabe cut for four. Again the English attack was losing ground against resolute players, one of them a dynamo of batsmanship. Bradman tapped a ball from Verity to Hammond, and apparently several women went into swoons; not for many days had I so much as this enjoyed cricket. It was skilful, antagonistic, vital; and the scene and the glorious day cast a splendour over all.

McCabe settled down after a vague beginning, and for the second time pulled Verity for four by the easiest back-stroke, and next ball drove a four to the off, upright and strong. The illusion of spin in Verity's bowling was going; England's urgent need was leg-spin. At lunch Australia had gripped the game once more.

Robins bowled after lunch. He had not seemed a dangerous bowler since he broke his spinning finger at Perth. The batting was admirable, with nothing reckless or rhetorical about it. Bradman and McCabe each watched the ball closely, played over the good ones, and annihilated the bad ones with rapid strokes, nearly all of them correct and good to see. Bradman put childish things behind him; never did he offend against taste, save when he attempted indiscreet, undignified singles. When he hooked, the ball was short and he was in charge of the direction.

McCabe hooked a no-ball from Voce with a forked lightning stroke, and the crack of his bat was the accompanying thunder. The stand was a comprehensive education in the organized technique of batting. Robins put Bradman into two minds, which was proof of a brilliant ball. In the same over McCabe pulled Robins hugely, and Wyatt at deep mid-wicket caught him at the third attempt. As the ball bounced in and out of Wyatt's hands, the heart of the crowd bounced, too, and Wyatt's face expressed changing agony, and my spectacles nearly came off.

Bradman now was all but run out because of Rigg's stupidity, and the night before I had dreamed he would be

run out. The crowd temporarily lost reason. And all these
stirring deeds were occurring in a beautiful scene, with the
hills and the cathedral spires the symbols of perfect peace.
Rigg apparently was determined to perform a run out, and
his first single was more or less demented, and so was his
second. Next minute there was another mix-up. An accurate
throw would have ended Rigg's lunacy, and an acrobatic
one would have ruined Bradman. The match had for the
moment turned gibbering.

Two fours off consecutive balls from Robins made Bradman 102, after three and a quarter hours of discipline, with
only six fours in all. It was an innings of most fell purpose.
At this point 14 were plundered from one over of Robins,
amid universal rejoicing. Bradman's fire blazed forth, now
threatening to consume England utterly. There is no argument about the name of the game's greatest match-winning
stroke-player when Bradman is Bradman.

Something was wrong with one of the bowling foot-
holds, and Allen prodded it with his feet, whereupon
Robins seized the bat from Rigg's clutches and dug the
earth; a sort of first gravedigger at somebody's funeral.
Rigg was caught prettily in the slips. His seven runs repre-
sented at least 70 palpitating crises. Young Gregory came in
next with Australia 195 ahead for four wickets. It was now
or never for either side; imps of caprice turned the game's
wheel hour by hour, and none of us knew where we were.
Had Gregory failed England might have won, after all. A
snick by Bradman eluded Verity at second slip; the bowler
was Hammond, and he at slip might have caught it. Twice
had Bradman to-day enjoyed luck, and he deserved to do
so. In the last over before tea a ball from Verity kept low,
and Bradman sliced it away to leg for nothing, but only a
great quick-sighted cricketer at the top of his form could

have eluded the beast. Bradman became austere whenever the game slightly veered England's way. The main point of his cricket was the generalship behind it all—he was playing for Australia, not for Bradman or for those people in the crowd who seem to look upon him as a sort of performing batsman, a virtuoso entertainer playing Paganini fireworks on a solo bat. He shielded Gregory, who none the less defended coolly, though without strokes. Moreover, the longer Bradman stayed in, the more the wicket was becoming amenable to Australia's spin bowlers, by the law of mundane perishability, which in the end will wear out the oldest rock, and even the foundations of the earth.

### FIFTH DAY

#### AUSTRALIA FIRST INNINGS

| | |
|---|---:|
| J. H. Fingleton, run out | 10 |
| W. A. Brown, c. Allen, b. Farnes | 42 |
| K. E. Rigg, c. Ames, b. Farnes | 20 |
| D. G. Bradman, b. Allen | 26 |
| S. J. McCabe, c. Allen, b. Robins | 88 |
| R. Gregory, l.b.w., b. Hammond | 23 |
| A. G. Chipperfield, not out | 57 |
| W. A. Oldfield, run out | 5 |
| W. J. O'Reilly, c. Leyland, b. Allen | 7 |
| E. L. McCormick, c. Ames, b. Hammond | 4 |
| L. O'B. Fleetwood-Smith, b. Farnes | 1 |
| Extras (l.b. 2, n.b. 3) | 5 |
| **Total** | **288** |

Australia first-innings bowling analysis

| | O. | M. | R. | W. |
|---|---:|---:|---:|---:|
| Voce | 12 | 0 | 49 | 0 |
| Allen | 16 | 0 | 60 | 2 |
| Farnes | 20·6 | 1 | 71 | 3 |
| Hammond | 6 | 0 | 30 | 2 |
| Verity | 16 | 4 | 47 | 0 |
| Robins | 7 | 1 | 26 | 1 |

Fall of the wickets:

| 1 | 2 | 3 | 4 | 5 | 6 | 7 | 8 | 9 | 10 |
|---|---|---|---|---|---|---|---|---|---|
| 26 | 72 | 73 | 136 | 206 | 226 | 249 | 271 | 283 | 288 |

## ENGLAND First Innings

| | |
|---|---|
| Barnett, l.b.w., b. Fleetwood-Smith . . . | 129 |
| Verity, c. Bradman, b. O'Reilly . . . | 19 |
| Hammond, c. McCormick, b. O'Reilly . . | 20 |
| Leyland, c. Chipperfield, b. Fleetwood-Smith . | 45 |
| R. E. S. Wyatt, c. Fingleton, b. O'Reilly . . | 3 |
| Ames, b. McCormick . . . . | 52 |
| Hardstaff, c. and b. McCormick . . . | 20 |
| G. O. Allen, l.b.w., b. Fleetwood-Smith . . | 11 |
| R. W. V. Robins, c. Oldfield, b. O'Reilly . | 10 |
| Voce, c. Rigg, b. Fleetwood-Smith . . . | 8 |
| K. Farnes, not out . . . . . | 0 |
| Extras (b. 6, l.b. 2, n.b. 4, w. 1) . . | 13 |
| Total . . . . . | 330 |

### England first-innings bowling analysis

| | O. | M. | R. | W. |
|---|---|---|---|---|
| McCormick . . | 21 | 2 | 81 | 2 |
| McCabe . . | 9 | 2 | 18 | 0 |
| Fleetwood-Smith . | 41·4 | 10 | 129 | 4 |
| O'Reilly . . | 30 | 12 | 51 | 4 |
| Chipperfield . . | 9 | 1 | 24 | 0 |
| Gregory . . | 3 | 0 | 14 | 0 |

### Fall of the wickets:

| 1 | 2 | 3 | 4 | 5 | 6 | 7 | 8 | 9 | 10 |
|---|---|---|---|---|---|---|---|---|---|
| 53 | 108 | 190 | 195 | 259 | 299 | 304 | 318 | 322 | 330 |

## AUSTRALIA Second Innings

| | |
|---|---|
| J. H. Fingleton, l.b.w., b. Hammond . . . | 12 |
| W. A. Brown, c. Ames, b. Voce . . | 32 |
| D. G. Bradman, c. and b. Hammond . . | 212 |
| S. J. McCabe, c. Wyatt, b. Robins . . | 55 |
| K. E. Rigg, c. Hammond, b. Farnes . . | 7 |
| R. Gregory, run out . . . . | 50 |
| A. G. Chipperfield, c. Ames, b. Hammond . | 31 |
| W. A. Oldfield, c. Ames, b. Hammond . | 1 |
| W. J. O'Reilly, c. Hammond, b. Farnes . | 1 |
| E. L. McCormick, b. Hammond . . | 1 |
| L. O'B. Fleetwood-Smith, not out . . | 4 |
| Extras (b. 10, l.b. 15, n.b. 1, w. 1) . | 27 |
| Total . . . . . | 433 |

Australia second-innings bowling analysis

|          | O. | M. | R. | W. |
|----------|-----|-----|-----|-----|
| Farnes . . . | 24 | 2 | 89 | 2 |
| Hammond . . | 15·2 | 1 | 57 | 5 |
| Allen . . . | 14 | 1 | 61 | 0 |
| Voce . . . | 20 | 2 | 86 | 1 |
| Verity . . . | 37 | 17 | 54 | 0 |
| Robins . . . | 6 | 0 | 38 | 1 |
| Barnett . . | 5 | 1 | 15 | 0 |
| Leyland . . | 2 | 0 | 6 | 0 |

Fall of the wickets:

| 1 | 2 | 3 | 4 | 5 | 6 | 7 | 8 | 9 | 10 |
|----|----|----|----|----|----|----|----|----|----|
| 21 | 88 | 197 | 237 | 372 | 422 | 426 | 427 | 429 | 433 |

ENGLAND Second Innings

| Verity, b. Fleetwood-Smith . . . . | 17 |
|---|---|
| Barnett, c. Chipperfield, b. Fleetwood-Smith . | 21 |
| Hardstaff, b. O'Reilly . . . . | 43 |
| Hammond, not out . . . . . | 39 |
| Leyland, not out . . . . . | 17 |
| Extras . . . . . . | 11 |
| Total (for 3 wickets) . . . . | 148 |

England second-innings bowling analysis to date

|          | O. | M. | R. | W. |
|----------|-----|-----|-----|-----|
| McCormick . . | 9 | 0 | 33 | 0 |
| McCabe . . | 3 | 0 | 9 | 0 |
| Fleetwood-Smith . | 17 | 1 | 60 | 2 |
| O'Reilly . . | 15 | 5 | 35 | 1 |

Fall of the wickets:

| 1 | 2 | 3 |
|----|----|----|
| 45 | 50 | 120 |

Hope for England is never vain, we assured ourselves, while Hammond is batting. At four o'clock the match seemed over. Fleetwood-Smith was bowling venomously, causing the pitch to behave like a fast, sticky one. Suddenly he lost sting, and possibly a change of ends was in some way the cause. I cannot believe the presence of Hammond upset him with memories of old, unhappy battles—for him —not so long ago. He is, at his best, the deadliest spin bowler in cricket. England temporarily emerged from the bodeful period with, of course, Hammond the calm stately man in charge. Hardstaff played his part and gave us recurrent flashes of his Nottinghamshire form until spin once again betrayed him.

The fifth morning began with Australia's position so secure that people in Adelaide were free to go and do some work with an easy conscience. I take it that whenever a Test match is in progress in Australia any form of work is a dereliction of duty. In the heavy steaming weather, Farnes bowled the first over, and at once found the edge of Bradman's bat—Heavens, it has one after all!—and beat Gregory with a ball which kept so low that none of the English fieldsmen could have been pleased to see it. Gregory played well again. I like Gregory; cricket is in his bones. He played a brave part in this match, and he won his spurs. Time will bring him an offside technique.

The pitch was still too good for England's style of attack; Farnes and Voce came through amiably, and Allen astonished us by calling on Leyland, as his first change, hoping, no doubt, that Leyland would bowl his Oriental ball known in Yorkshire as the 'chinaman', the quaint left-handed googly, which Emmott Robinson regarded with suspicion from his place at silly point. Also, Leyland was probably used as an experiment with the new leg-before-wicket rule. In his first over he did not consistently hit the pitch at all, and he surveyed his own efforts with humour.

Allen attacked with all his heart; the leg-spin bowler needed by England does not exist in England at the present day, for on English wickets simple finger-break is encouraged, and there is no compulsion on a cricketer to learn the heart-breaking job of turning over his arm and wrist strenuously at the risk of sending a two-bouncer. Gregory's innings came to a startling end. He pushed Allen to long on, and Barnett pursued the stroke; the second run made Gregory's score 50, and Barnett threw him out when a third run was almost completed. Barnett's swift pick-up and return deserved Bradman himself as a reward.

When Bradman was 199, Verity bowled over the wicket to an appropriately arranged field; the plan clearly was to get Bradman run out, or caught, trying what cricketers call a 'tickle to leg' for his 200. He declined the bait, and next over he hit Voce for three to the on, easy and confident as a player in the nets. Thus the greatest of batsmen kept the appointment with a double century which on Monday he came forth to keep. The journey was long for Bradman, but he travelled by Pullman, plush cushions and all. The precision of his cricket was so unfaltering that I began to wonder whether he could get himself out, even by trying hard. I thought of a short story which I have never yet been able to find time to write, about a girl trapeze artist who, disappointed in love, decides one night to crash in front of the crowded audience and break her neck, but cannot crash because she is enslaved to a perfect technique.

Chipperfield again scored dapper runs. Indeed, when Verity was not bowling over the wicket more or less negatively, the English bowling was palpably at its wits' ends. Bradman actually committed a mortal error five minutes from lunch, returning a ball to Hammond in the act of aiming straight at the boundary. The innings was a compendium or encyclopedia of batsmanship. In it the fine fruits of past skill blossomed from the soil of contemporary cricket. It was a wonderful piece of sustained cleverness and generalship.

After lunch, Hammond took quick wickets, and we could see again how easily Australia would have lost the rubber if Bradman had failed. I believe that England without Hammond would have defeated Australia without Bradman. But that is beside the point, which is that Bradman was Australia's backbone and nerve-centre. Hammond came through a long innings with a remarkable if rather flattering bowling analysis. None the less, he was not, on such a wicket, used enough; Allen probably wished, in the sultry weather, to conserve as much as he could the energies of his best batsman. Before England's innings began, the lightest roller was employed. Verity, by the way, did not give a run away to-day; he wheeled up eight overs for none and for nothing.

The radio played Franz Lehar's 'Vilia' song from *The Merry Widow* while the umpires walked out. I have heard the music in many places between Vienna and the Midland Hotel, Manchester, where the string orchestra of Drescher played it in the old days; I never expected to hear it at Adelaide when England had their backs to the wall. McCormick bowled at splendid pace with the new ball, and a rising ball nearly got Barnett caught in the slips from a jerked protective stab. At the wicket's other end, McCabe also sent down the new ball more or less ritualistically, and Verity, in first for England once more, played a dignified straight bat, and scored 10 to Barnett's 4. These, of course, were preliminary skirmishes before the spin bowlers got into action.

Another kicker by McCormick was shielded by Barnett's bat; it came up at a sharp angle, and Barnett would have been unlucky to be caught at short mid-on. Barnett then was missed off Fleetwood-Smith from a drive straight to Fingleton at mid-off, an easy chance. This was one of the few catches missed by Australia in the rubber. The next ball was driven dashingly for four; from the next a short single was stolen, amid screams, and the next ball baffled and bowled Verity all over the place.

Hardstaff, not Hammond, went in first wicket down, and only his lucky stars saved him. First ball, a spinner on the middle stump, passed the off stump, fizzing gorgeously. In Fleetwood-Smith's subsequent over Barnett was caught at slip by Chipperfield. He tried a forward drive, and the going-away break suggested a fast, sticky wicket. This was the ideal bowling for the dry earth; natural genius; deadly unplayable revolutions, quick as a top off the ground, and exquisitely flighted, with the sinuous curve of temptation. Hardstaff was missed at mid-on by McCormick off O'Reilly as soon as Hammond arrived. Consternation throbbed in the English ranks, and Hammond tried a savage cut at Fleetwood-Smith.

After tea McCormick was put on at the end from which Fleetwood-Smith had awakened havoc; Fleetwood-Smith crossed over. At once the batting regained composure. Hardstaff made clean purposeful strokes against the fast stuff. I doubted the wisdom of this change; a bowler in form should not alter his base of attack. Fleetwood-Smith lost sting suddenly, and Hardstaff pulled a long-hop powerfully, a stroke of grandeur. His innings acquired style, confidence, quickness of vision and mind. At last he promised a resurrection. O'Reilly was called back, and Fleetwood-Smith returned to the end where before tea he had threatened a quick end to the issue.

A masterful cover-drive by Hammond off O'Reilly temporarily cleared the air for England, but in Fleetwood-Smith's first over when he bowled at the other and right end, Hardstaff pulled viciously at a short ball, and O'Reilly almost made the catch of his career at short mid-on. It was a severe chance.

I have seldom known the atmosphere of an innings to lighten and emerge from crisis to some assurance as the English innings did between four o'clock and five. Hardstaff, allowed by mistakes in the field to find himself, batted better than he had batted before in this rubber. Now the crowd were able, perhaps, to understand why we think much of this cricketer in England, though even now he was playing only at half-pressure, so to say. Care bowed him down still. He was bowled by O'Reilly at twenty-five past five, by a ball which clearly turned not at all according to Hardstaff's expectations.

The Australian fielding was at its best and most vehement.

## SIXTH DAY

### AUSTRALIA First Innings

| | |
|---|---:|
| J. H. Fingleton, run out . . . . | 10 |
| W. A. Brown, c. Allen, b. Farnes . . | 42 |
| K. E. Rigg, c. Ames, b. Farnes . . . | 20 |
| D. G. Bradman, b. Allen . . . . | 26 |
| S. J. McCabe, c. Allen, b. Robins . . | 88 |
| R. Gregory, l.b.w., b. Hammond . . | 23 |
| A. G. Chipperfield, not out . . . | 57 |
| W. A. Oldfield, run out . . . . | 5 |
| W. J. O'Reilly, c. Leyland, b. Allen . . | 7 |
| E. L. McCormick, c. Ames, b. Hammond . | 4 |
| L. O'B. Fleetwood-Smith, b. Farnes . . | 1 |
| Extras (l.b. 2, n.b. 3) . . . . | 5 |
| Total . . . . . | 288 |

Australia first-innings bowling analysis

| | O. | M. | R. | W. |
|---|---|---|---|---|
| Voce . . . | 12 | 0 | 49 | 0 |
| Allen . . . | 16 | 0 | 60 | 2 |
| Farnes . . . | 20·6 | 1 | 71 | 3 |
| Hammond . . | 6 | 0 | 30 | 2 |
| Verity . . . | 16 | 4 | 47 | 0 |
| Robins . . | 7 | 1 | 26 | 1 |

## Fall of the wickets:

| 1 | 2 | 3 | 4 | 5 | 6 | 7 | 8 | 9 | 10 |
|---|---|---|---|---|---|---|---|---|----|
| 26 | 72 | 73 | 136 | 206 | 226 | 249 | 271 | 283 | 288 |

## ENGLAND First Innings

| | | |
|---|---|---:|
| Barnett, l.b.w., b. Fleetwood-Smith | . . | 129 |
| Verity, c. Bradman, b. O'Reilly . | . . | 19 |
| Hammond, c. McCormick, b. O'Reilly | . | 20 |
| Leyland, c. Chipperfield, b. Fleetwood-Smith | . | 45 |
| R. E. S. Wyatt, c. Fingleton, b. O'Reilly | . | 3 |
| Ames, b. McCormick | . . | 52 |
| Hardstaff, c. and b. McCormick . | . | 20 |
| G. O. Allen, l.b.w., b. Fleetwood-Smith | . | 11 |
| R. W. V. Robins, c. Oldfield, b. O'Reilly . | | 10 |
| Voce, c. Rigg, b. Fleetwood-Smith | . . | 8 |
| K. Farnes, not out . . . . | . . | 0 |
| Extras (b. 6, l.b. 2, n.b. 4, w. 1) . | . | 13 |
| Total . . . . | . | 330 |

### England first-innings bowling analysis

| | O. | M. | R. | W. |
|---|---|---|---|---|
| McCormick . . | 21 | 2 | 81 | 2 |
| McCabe . . | 9 | 2 | 18 | 0 |
| Fleetwood-Smith . | 41·4 | 10 | 129 | 4 |
| O'Reilly . . | 30 | 12 | 51 | 4 |
| Chipperfield . . | 9 | 1 | 24 | 0 |
| Gregory . . | 3 | 0 | 14 | 0 |

### Fall of the wickets:

| 1 | 2 | 3 | 4 | 5 | 6 | 7 | 8 | 9 | 10 |
|---|---|---|---|---|---|---|---|---|----|
| 53 | 108 | 190 | 195 | 259 | 299 | 304 | 318 | 322 | 330 |

## AUSTRALIA Second Innings

| | | |
|---|---|---:|
| J. H. Fingleton, l.b.w., b. Hammond . | . | 12 |
| W. A. Brown, c. Ames, b. Voce | . | 32 |
| D. G. Bradman, c. and b. Hammond . | . | 212 |
| S. J. McCabe, c. Wyatt, b. Robins | . | 55 |
| K. E. Rigg, c. Hammond, b. Farnes . | . | 7 |
| R. Gregory, run out . . . | . | 50 |
| A. G. Chipperfield, c. Ames, b. Hammond . | | 31 |
| W. A. Oldfield, c. Ames, b. Hammond | . | 1 |

## AUSTRALIA Second Innings—*continued*

W. J. O'Reilly, c. Hammond, b. Farnes . . 1
E. L. McCormick, b. Hammond. . . . 1
L. O'B. Fleetwood-Smith, not out . . . 4
    Extras (b. 10, l.b. 15, n.b. 1, w. 1) . . 27
                                                   —
    Total . . . . . 433

### Australia second-innings bowling analysis

|  | O. | M. | R. | W. |
|---|---|---|---|---|
| Farnes . . . | 24 | 2 | 89 | 2 |
| Hammond . . | 15·2 | 1 | 57 | 5 |
| Allen . . . | 14 | 1 | 61 | 0 |
| Voce . . . | 20 | 2 | 86 | 1 |
| Verity . . . | 37 | 17 | 54 | 0 |
| Robins . . . | 6 | 0 | 38 | 1 |
| Barnett . . | 5 | 1 | 15 | 0 |
| Leyland . . | 2 | 0 | 6 | 0 |

### Fall of the wickets:

| 1 | 2 | 3 | 4 | 5 | 6 | 7 | 8 | 9 | 10 |
|---|---|---|---|---|---|---|---|---|---|
| 21 | 88 | 197 | 237 | 372 | 422 | 426 | 427 | 429 | 433 |

### ENGLAND Second Innings

Verity, b. Fleetwood-Smith . . . 17
Barnett, c. Chipperfield, b. Fleetwood-Smith . 21
Hardstaff, b. O'Reilly . . . . 43
Hammond, b. Fleetwood-Smith . . 39
Leyland, c. Chipperfield, b. Fleetwood-Smith 32
R. E. S. Wyatt, c. Oldfield, b. McCabe . . 50
Ames, l.b.w., b. Fleetwood-Smith . . . 0
G. O. Allen, c. Gregory, b. McCormick . . 9
R. W. V. Robins, b. McCormick . . 4
Voce, b. Fleetwood-Smith . . . 1
K. Farnes, not out . . . . . 7
    Extras (b. 12, l.b. 2, n.b. 6) . . . 20
                                                   —
    Total . . . . . 243

### England second-innings bowling analysis

|  | O. | M. | R. | W. |
|---|---|---|---|---|
| McCormick . . | 13 | 1 | 43 | 2 |
| McCabe . . | 5 | 0 | 15 | 1 |
| Fleetwood-Smith . | 30 | 1 | 110 | 6 |
| O'Reilly . . | 26 | 8 | 55 | 1 |

Fall of the wickets:

| 1 | 2 | 3 | 4 | 5 | 6 | 7 | 8 | 9 | 10 |
|---|---|---|---|---|---|---|---|---|----|
| 45 | 50 | 120 | 149 | 190 | 190 | 225 | 231 | 235 | 243 |

Fleetwood-Smith won the match by wonderful spin. He quickly overwhelmed Hammond, Leyland, and Ames with balls deadly in their swift break, and beautiful in their seductive curve through the air. The wicket was his accomplice, though to most other bowlers it would have helped only now and again. I cannot imagine the batsmen who could have avoided for long the snares of Fleetwood-Smith. It can hardly be said that England collapsed. They got out by the inexorable law of cause and effect.

No cricketer has yet evolved a technique which will cope with the quick spinning-away ball. The only criticism that might with some lack of charity be passed on the English batsmen is that they did not often use quick feet and jump to kill the break at birth. Fleetwood-Smith has three tricks for the bewildering of his antagonists—his googly is waspish, and is hard to discover; he also bowls a topspinner, and the lefthander's usual break across from leg. In this engagement he mingled these tricks craftily, and kept a length good enough to make his long-hops and full tosses most artful blandishments.

In the morning's first over Fleetwood-Smith practically settled the issue. A lovely ball lured Hammond forward, broke at the critical length, evaded the bat, and bowled England's pivot and main hope. The crowd roared out their joy, and sent three cheers into the sunshine for Fleetwood-Smith, while Bradman ran to him and shook his hand.

This achievement set a crown on the most skilful and artistic spin bowler of the day. I know of no rarer beauty in cricket than the slow spinning ball which compels a great batsman to reach forward against his inclinations, and whips across even as his bat gropes in the void.

Fleetwood-Smith bowled two bad lengths to Wyatt, who smote them gratefully. Some purist in the crowd stated that Fleetwood-Smith's trouble is that he often pitches too short or too full. But this is the secret of his ability to worry the finest defence. His bad bowling can never really be trusted. At any moment he is likely to spin an unplayable masterpiece. To folk who love cricket for other than competitive reasons, the capriciousness of Fleetwood-Smith's attack is a constant delight. Test matches are nowadays more or less in the control of precise mechanics who usually know what they are doing because they are attempting little and seldom venturing into the regions of the fantastic, or even the uncommon.

Wyatt batted confidently and well, while Leyland was the image of Yorkshire obstinacy. Another glorious ball from Fleetwood-Smith flashed so rapidly past Leyland's forward bat that it fizzed away before it could be touched. In each over Fleetwood-Smith sent a ball which was good enough for Bradman himself, a beauty before it pitched, a work of genius considered in the abstract, quite apart from its utility value, or its power to get a wicket. Perfect art, as Oscar Wilde said, is absolutely useless.

Wyatt jumped into a half-volley from Fleetwood-Smith, and drove it along the ground for three. Wyatt was in excellent form, and at his best he is good to look at, correct and thoughtful, and a respecter of the unities—that sort of general oneness, as the gentleman in Dickens put it.

Several times in the match an England batsman succumbed just as a good stand seemed to be ripening. Fleetwood-Smith spun away once more, this time from Leyland's bat, and Chipperfield held the inevitable catch. The

next ball confounded Ames, who was leg-before, hoping
for the best. Whenever Fleetwood-Smith dropped a slow
alluring length, the ball as it struck the dry earth changed
the pitch to a fast 'sticky dog', as cricketers say. The bowling was inspired by the evil spirit of the grotesque. I have
seldom seen bowling more incalculable and original than
this. The game was now ready for the accountancy of the
scorers. Allen survived incredibly until lunch. He was perhaps carrying next to his heart an amulet, some Oriental
charm against mortal wounds. He persistently got up after
he had been pierced fatally. He was plucky and would not
die.

O'Reilly found the pitch so unhelpful that in vain he
tried to spin for eighty-five minutes. He then resorted to
methods which asked for the collaboration of the leg trap.
Fleetwood-Smith alone could evoke the demons hidden in
the ground. And Wyatt continued his exposition of the
ABC of batting. He parsed and analysed every over. His
form was a real consolation to England in a distressful
situation.

After lunch the new ball was employed by McCormick
and McCabe, and at once Allen was caught trying a forcing
hit. Wyatt's admirable innings came to an end when Oldfield caught him off a ball from McCabe, which came
quickly from the pitch. And subsequent proceedings interested me no more. The agony will begin anew at Melbourne, we said. And it did.

# CHAPTER XIV

# FIFTH TEST—MELBOURNE

*February 26—March 3, 1937*

## *FIRST DAY*

### AUSTRALIA First Innings

| | | |
|---|---|---:|
| J. H. Fingleton, c. Voce, b. Farnes | . . . | 17 |
| K. E. Rigg, c. Ames, b. Farnes | . . . | 28 |
| D. G. Bradman, not out | . . . . | 165 |
| S. J. McCabe, c. Farnes, b. Verity | . . | 112 |
| C. L. Badcock, not out | . . . . | 12 |
| Extras (b. 1, l.b. 2, n.b. 4, w. 1) | . . . | 8 |

Total (for 3 wickets) . . . . 342

To bat.—R. Gregory, L. O'B. Fleetwood-Smith, E. L. McCormick, W. A. Oldfield, W. J. O'Reilly, and L. J. Nash.

Australia first-innings bowling analysis to date

| | O. | M. | R. | W. |
|---|---|---|---|---|
| Allen . . . | 12 | 0 | 72 | 0 |
| Farnes . . . | 13 | 3 | 45 | 2 |
| Voce . . . | 13 | 2 | 68 | 0 |
| Hammond . . | 10 | 1 | 44 | 0 |
| Verity . . . | 14 | 0 | 68 | 1 |
| Worthington . . | 2 | 0 | 21 | 0 |
| Leyland . . | 2 | 0 | 16 | 0 |

Fall of the wickets:

| 1 | 2 | 3 |
|---|---|---|
| 42 | 54 | 303 |

A GREAT stand by Bradman and McCabe gave Australia a grip on the rubber. It occurred in time to save the match from the threat of mechanical dreariness; and a missed catch by Allen, when McCabe's innings was merely in the bud, changed the day's course.

Bradman again was a wonder of precision and reserved power. He attempted nothing that custom has not told him he can do safely and fruitfully. He was never uninteresting. He merely abstained from vanity and rhetoric. The England attack, as I hope to emphasize later, mistakenly relied on pace. The Melbourne wicket belied its past, and the day was a batsman's friend and supporter. But the England fast bowlers did little to exploit whatever the wicket had in it before lunch to aid and abet the rising, and lawfully rising, ball.

Leg-spin would have come as a boon and a blessing to Allen, but truth to say—as I have already insisted—there is not in English cricket at the moment a single leg-spin bowler of Australian ability. English wickets encourage conventional pace, new ball shibboleths, and the finger-spin of hoary tradition. Farnes bowled admirably and was alone.

It was a broiling day. The great crowd, heaped up rank on rank, took on a swollen shape and personality of its own—a squatting Moloch ready to feed on the cricketers' hopes and frustrations. And the brown wicket lay in the heat like a block of execution on which reputations soon would receive the axe and, perhaps not without relief, give up the ghost. A roar of delight announced that Bradman had won the toss. Allen shrugged his shoulders fatalistically.

Allen's second ball reared on the offside past Fingleton's nose, and shortly we saw Allen down on his knee attending to his bootlaces. Farnes, not Voce, bowled at the other end with the new ball. He, too, obtained vivacity from the earth, and from the last ball of his second over, Fingleton hurriedly glanced low and straight to Allen, who missed the chance with signs of self-flagellation. It was, for Test cricket, an easy chance.

A pretty late glance by Rigg off Allen was the day's opening boundary. Rigg shaped like a good and confident batsman, ready to bide his time, yet ready to put forth excellent strokes to the convenient ball. Voce attacked instead of Allen at the end of twenty-five minutes. The pitch was already losing resilience, and Hammond went on for Farnes. Voce could not make the ball rise higher than the upper region of the stumps and at a quarter to one the batsmen were defending at their leisure. In imagination I saw the match assuming a sort of ponderous slow-moving bulk. Modern Test cricket seems as much related to hazardous sport as modern trench warfare to the ancient lance and tournament.

The heat smote the field from a sky of unstained blue in which a single white cloud was as still as an island of the blessed. The bowlers toiled on the cruel pitch, the crowd perspired rivulets, the batsmen and fieldsmen snatched at flies.

Suddenly Rigg hooked Allen for four, and lifted Australia's total to 32 in an hour, by which time Fingleton had dutifully refrained from scoring more than six. In circumstances born for strokes and cricket, none but an accomplished Test match player could bat an hour for six. At a quarter-past one Verity bowled, and Fingleton drove or pushed his first ball in front of point for four—compelled to the stroke, no doubt, by the eternal law of action and reaction that governs the changing tides.

Ten minutes before lunch England made an advance. Farnes, who was easily the best bowler, got Rigg caught at the wicket. In the same over, Bradman drove twice for two off the back foot; the balls were so admirable in length that only a Bradman in form could have done much more than stop them during his preliminary moments at the crease. The advent of Bradman was a breeze coming into the doldrums.

From the second ball after lunch, Fingleton leaned across to an offside ball, and steered it accurately to the slips. This was self-destruction as clear and unmistakable as any occurrence in a gas oven with a passionate farewell letter left on the mantelpiece. McCabe immediately smote a no-ball from Voce to the on. So far the English fast bowling had been a pattern of gentlemanliness, no short stuff on principle. Yet if fast bowlers had never pitched short in cricket's long history, how could the hook stroke have been practised and developed? Persistent fast bowling to a leg-field is one thing; the occasional short one to keep a batsman awake is another matter altogether.

Farnes made a noble effort to catch and bowl Bradman. He fell forward and missed by a foot. The deed will be recorded by the angels who do not go by results. Now a terrible thing occurred; McCabe was 11 only when he turned Farnes round to short leg, where Allen could thrust only one hand to the chance. Had the catch been held it would not have seemed extraordinary. This was the last straw and it broke our backs.

Accurate bowling and responsibility caused Bradman to check his hits for a long while, but he looked thoroughly at ease, and content to admire a number of charming strokes by McCabe. Two glorious fours to the off from Allen took Bradman to 50 in a little over an hour. On the face of it he had played defensively, which only proves that a batsman with strokes is able to score on a perfect wicket at a good pace and yet not risk his wicket in the slightest. The average modern batsman scores slowly not because he will not, but because he cannot, go faster.

The game flared up when Worthington came on.

Fourteen were hit in an over. I felt we were at the critical point of the innings, perhaps of the match. If England failed to take another wicket at once the bowling would be lucky not to be mastered and bruised by Australia's greatest batsmen. Already England were feeling the want of spin, or the ball that gets a player out before it pitches. McCabe's batting was fluent and gracious. There is no effort, no wasted energy in his movements; he was in perfect contrast to Bradman, who is essentially a dynamic player. McCabe is all curves of style. The difference between McCabe and Bradman is the difference between the rapier and sword, or, to change the figure, between the aristocrat and the man of the people. Leyland bowled at ten to four. England's attack had called up the reserves; the enemy were advancing all along the line.

After tea Bradman reached yet another hundred in Test matches, after only two hours' batting. He hit only seven fours while making it. At half-pressure Bradman is the quickest long-distance scorer of the day. His performances in these games stagger credulity. No writer of boys' fiction would dare to invent a hero who approached, let alone equalled, Bradman's persistent centuries and double and triple centuries. He would be charged by the critics with going beyond even a fantastic heroism. I wonder if Bradman ever grows tired of his own mastery and sighs for new worlds to conquer, new reaches of achievement outside the great capacity of his skill. Or is he satisfied to go on being humanly acquisitive? To-day he caused batting to appear as easy and as natural as breathing, walking, or eating.

The moment he reached the wicket the match became touched with genius, and McCabe kept in the picture as well. There were strokes to enjoy now; this was the cricket we had waited for, and feared would not come.

The England attack lost what little of antagonism it had known at the day's beginning. It is in vain to try to defeat a flawless Australian pitch by pace alone; and England's fast bowlers were not even fast. Farnes, the ablest of the three, seldom got beyond fast-medium.

McCabe gave another chance, this time to Farnes at forward leg. Missed catches are part of cricket, maybe, but England were overstepping a reasonable margin of error, with two consummate batsmen thoroughly set. McCabe's hundred was reached, amid great acclamation. In spite of his two chances he gave us an exquisite display of his own lissome art. There is no batsman to-day better worth watching than McCabe, unless it is Woolley, now alas coming to the end of his career.

McCabe was out just before half-past five. His stand with Bradman put up a new record for the third wicket in Test matches. Better still, the stand gave Australia a strong grip of the rubber. Bradman and McCabe scored 249 in two hours and forty minutes; finer batsmanship could not well be imagined than this. Both players served Australia in a responsible moment, and, better still, served the arts and graces of cricket.

---

## SECOND DAY

### AUSTRALIA First Innings

| | |
|---|---:|
| J. H. Fingleton, c. Voce, b. Farnes . . . | 17 |
| K. E. Rigg, c. Ames, b. Farnes . . . . | 28 |
| D. G. Bradman, b. Farnes . . . | 169 |
| S. J. McCabe, c. Farnes, b. Verity . . | 112 |
| C. L. Badcock, c. Worthington, b. Voce . | 118 |
| R. Gregory, c. Verity, b. Farnes . . . | 80 |
| W. A. Oldfield, c. Ames, b. Voce . . . | 21 |
| L. J. Nash, c. Ames, b. Farnes . . . . | 17 |
| W. J. O'Reilly, b. Voce . . . . . | 1 |
| E. L. McCormick, not out . . . . | 9 |

AUSTRALIA First Innings—*continued*

L. O'B. Fleetwood-Smith, not out . . . 11
Extras (b. 1, l.b. 4, n.b. 4, w. 1) . . . 10

Total (for 9 wickets) . . . . 593

Australia first-innings bowling analysis to date

|            | O. | M. | R. | W. |
|------------|----|----|----|----|
| Allen . . . | 17 | 0 | 99 | 0 |
| Farnes . . . | 27 | 5 | 92 | 5 |
| Voce . . . | 27 | 3 | 117 | 3 |
| Hammond . . | 16 | 1 | 62 | 0 |
| Verity . . . | 41 | 3 | 127 | 1 |
| Worthington . . | 6 | 0 | 60 | 0 |
| Leyland . . | 3 | 0 | 26 | 0 |

Fall of the wickets:

| 1 | 2 | 3 | 4 | 5 | 6 | 7 | 8 | 9 |
|----|----|----|----|----|----|----|----|----|
| 42 | 54 | 303 | 346 | 507 | 544 | 563 | 571 | 576 |

Australia forced home Friday's advantage, in spite of a quick end this morning to Bradman. Two cricketers, more or less new to Test matches, batted with ease and delight. Badcock's innings told of the coming of yet another stroke-player of the great Australian succession. I am astonished that many English critics still seem to associate Australian batsmen with slow scoring. It is not by accident that the only hundreds scored before lunch in matches between England and Australia have been by Australians— Trumper, Macartney, Bradman. The Australian batsman as a rule hits the loose ball.

England bowled determinedly, and Farnes deserved his remarkable analysis. He alone consistently made the batsmen think of the likelihood of a perilous ball coming along quick from the ground. But it was fool-hardy of England to take the field without leg-spin, even the leg-spin of Sims, which often remains an idea in the mind of Sims.

To win the rubber now, England required extraordinary batting and a sticky wicket during Australia's second innings. If England lost the rubber, we agreed, little good would be done by blaming the English selection committee. It is not their fault that great leg-spin bowlers are not bred in a land where rain, or some sort óf moisture, is always encouraging an easier way of obtaining wickets. There is a difference between finger-spin, and wrist-plus-finger-spin. Even Freeman could not turn the ball in Australia.

The brilliant morning was cooled by a gentle wind, and all Melbourne seemed to be going to the Test match: men, women, boys and girls, the Government, the income tax including an oldest inhabitant. A bird's-eye view would have shown the population being sucked into the round space of the cricket ground like water down the hole of a bath. If H. M. Bateman had been in Melbourne, he would probably have drawn a picture of the man who, on a Test match occasion, asked a policeman the nearest way to the Art Gallery. The drawing would depict the adjacent trees and spires and what-not all twisting and gyrating with indignation.

On a wicket good enough for a batsman's magic carpet on which he might ride to the loftiest regions, Bradman and Badcock went on with Australia's innings; the crowd, insatiable ever, prepared for more and more boundaries from the master. He was bowled in the second over of Farnes, trying a pull from a ball a little too high for the stroke, and swift as light from the ground. I was beginning to think that Bradman was not to be bowled by mortal effort. This innings had about it the air of complete control, with technique not a servant of the mind but the outward and swift manifestation of the mind itself.

Bradman's secret is abnormal concentration; and the ability to get closer to the ball than any cricketer since Ranjitsinhji. He can score 60 runs an hour with the sound wide bat of the stonewaller. In this innings he put aside all skittishness, all vanity, and played for Australia. This was the master linking freedom to taste and proportion.

After a dubious stroke or two against Farnes, Badcock began to hook vehemently, and Hardstaff again gave chase. In the gruelling heat, he chased hour after hour, a gallant sight with his fair hair and his smile to the crowd when the ball beat him inches from the boundary. Barnett also saved a four at top speed. There was a keen aggressive note in the England team now. A last-minute effort was going on, to retrieve the dangerous situation. Badcock began most ominously to look as if Bradman had made and shaped him and breathed fire into him. Sometimes Badcock drove from the back foot so like Bradman that I felt that the English captain should have insisted, as they say at elections, on a recount. Here is another great Australian batsman in the making, and nearly made, a stroke-player, not a slave of the push and poke.

The excellent fact about Australia's innings was the manner of their escape from Friday's bad start and doldrums. The recovery was done by strokes, real batsmanship. I hoped England would follow the example, because the policy of staying in regardless of runs is dangerous, as we saw at Adelaide. Where no time limit exists in a match, there is little point in beating the clock. The steadiest innings will come to an end sooner or later; and then it is the runs made that count.

Gregory played well and coolly. A forcing stroke in front of the wicket off Allen for three was effortless, all wrists and balance. Then Badcock cut Allen late with the pretty intimate touch of J. T. Brown. Australia were on top once more, giving us beautiful cricket, cricket diademed with cuts and drives. And now two youngsters were doing it all. Generation succeeds unto generation.

The England attack, though steady, lacked spin, swerve, great pace, and venom in general. Verity did his best to exploit variation of flight and pace, but on the beautiful pitch his close abstract thinking remained more or less abstract.

Correct length by Verity checked the ardour of Badcock and Gregory in the half-hour before lunch. The rotary persistence of Verity's overs numbed the senses, and they needed some numbing, for the crowd was enormous and the women's noises were fearful. Farnes was again England's best bowler, and when the Australian score stood at 418 for four, Farnes had taken three wickets for 62. He kept a length, and occasionally he made speed from the ground. The stroke by which Badcock reached 50, an impulsive slash through the slips, was morally another wicket for Farnes. Another superb drive to the off from the back foot related Badcock closer than first cousin to Bradman; and in the same over a four to the off by Badcock was one of the best hits of the match.

I had known, ever since I first saw Badcock in the nets at Perth in October, that he was the third finest batsman in Australia. Would he were an Englishman! Badcock hereabout scored from almost every ball, and another slash through the slips, this time off Allen, momentarily spoiled a splendid innings.

A number of capital shots by Gregory only lacked power to make them as profitable as stylish. This power will come. Australia is lucky to possess these two young men, both full of cricket. When Worthington bowled, two indiscreet snicks or slashes by Gregory eluded the slips, but scarcely deserved to escape poetic justice. All things considered, the English bowlers and fielders stuck to their task gamely. Little or nothing was given away.

Amid tumultuous cheerings, Badcock reached his first Test match century by a dashing drive off Verity—his first, but not his last. I have seldom watched with more pleasure a young player getting his foot on the rungs of the ladder of international cricket. Badcock will adorn the game for years to come, and give pleasure to crowds here and at the other end of the world. Another burst of cheering announced Gregory's 50. This stand was youth's retort to the charge that 'when Don's out, we're all out'. Badcock's innings ended in the manner I expected. He was caught in the slips, stabbing at a ball which probably went away. He was roared back to the pavilion, and the women gazed at him adoringly.

Gregory welcomed Oldfield with a gloriously upright straight drive. Heaven bless us! We have again witnessed strokes in a Test match, gay and handsome and cultured strokes. Gregory failed by twenty to get his hundred; he was caught at forward leg. It was a likable innings, a little short of resource and masculinity, but most promising in its defence, composure, and judgment.

Clouds were stealing across the sky now, and a shower of rain fell. Allen looked at the heavens ironically. His cup would overflow if once again his team were trapped on a Melbourne sticky pitch. No true cricketer wished such a dreadful recurrence. When Australia's total was 530 Ames had allowed only one bye. He is to-day worth his place in an England team for wicket-keeping alone. A circumspect stand by Oldfield and Nash, at the afternoon's fall, provided, I think, a case of playing the game for England, who

surely did not wish to bat for any length of time in the
closing period, with the light not too good.

## THIRD DAY

### AUSTRALIA First Innings

| | |
|---|---:|
| J. H. Fingleton, c. Voce, b. Farnes . . . | 17 |
| K. E. Rigg, c. Ames, b. Farnes . . . . | 28 |
| D. G. Bradman, b. Farnes . . . . | 169 |
| S. J. McCabe, c. Farnes, b. Verity . . . | 112 |
| C. L. Badcock, c. Worthington, b. Voce . | 118 |
| R. Gregory, c. Verity, b. Farnes . . . | 80 |
| W. A. Oldfield, c. Ames, b. Voce . . . | 21 |
| L. J. Nash, c. Ames, b. Farnes . . . | 17 |
| W. J. O'Reilly, b. Voce . . . . . | 1 |
| E. L. McCormick, not out . . . . | 17 |
| L. O'B. Fleetwood-Smith, b. Farnes . . | 13 |
| Extras (b. 1, l.b. 5, n.b. 4, w. 1) . . . | 11 |
| Total . . . . . . | 604 |

### Australia first-innings bowling analysis

| | O. | M. | R. | W. |
|---|---|---|---|---|
| Allen . . . | 17 | 0 | 99 | 0 |
| Farnes . . . | 28·5 | 5 | 96 | 6 |
| Voce . . . | 29 | 3 | 123 | 3 |
| Hammond . . | 16 | 1 | 62 | 0 |
| Verity . . . | 41 | 5 | 127 | 1 |
| Worthington . . | 6 | 0 | 60 | 0 |
| Leyland . . | 3 | 0 | 26 | 0 |

### Fall of the wickets:

| 1 | 2 | 3 | 4 | 5 | 6 | 7 | 8 | 9 | 10 |
|---|---|---|---|---|---|---|---|---|---|
| 32 | 54 | 303 | 346 | 507 | 544 | 563 | 571 | 576 | 604 |

### ENGLAND First Innings

| | |
|---|---:|
| Barnett, c. Oldfield, b. Nash . . . . | 18 |
| Worthington, hit wicket, b. Fleetwood-Smith . | 44 |
| Hardstaff, not out . . . . . . | 73 |
| Hammond, c. Nash, b. O'Reilly . . . | 14 |
| Leyland, b. O'Reilly . . . . . | 7 |
| R. E. S. Wyatt, not out . . . . . | 20 |
| Extras . . . . . . . | 8 |
| Total (for 4 wickets) . . . . | 184 |

To bat.—Ames, G. O. Allen, Voce, K. Farnes, and Verity.

England first-innings bowling analysis to date

|  | O. | M. | R. | W. |
|---|---|---|---|---|
| McCormick . . | 8·2 | 1 | 32 | 0 |
| Nash . . . | 13 | 0 | 60 | 1 |
| O'Reilly . . | 17 | 6 | 33 | 2 |
| Fleetwood-Smith . | 18 | 3 | 51 | 1 |

Fall of the wickets:

| 1 | 2 | 3 | 4 |
|---|---|---|---|
| 33 | 96 | 130 | 140 |

On the easiest wicket I have seen, and one on which steadiness in a bowler was a virtue, England's batting disappointed grievously. The innings began incoherently; Barnett appeared to be under the impression that he was playing at Cheltenham in a picnic engagement. Hammond got himself out absent-mindedly after a strokeless innings which disquieted me, and Leyland allowed a good length ball to beat him.

A stand by Worthington and Hardstaff for the second wicket promised well, but Worthington trod on his stumps while making an excellent hit. He was exhibiting his Derbyshire form. Hardstaff alone conducted himself with a great player's assurance and style. He at last announced his quality to Australia.

The Australian bowling could not, in the conditions, be deadly, though it had the variety of flight and pace which were absent from England's. The fielding, too, was keen and reliable, on the whole. I could account for the moderate batting only in terms of the vast score facing England. English cricketers are not accustomed to going in against 600. But there must be no unfair criticism of Allen. He worked magnificently with a team which revealed serious defects from the beginning of the tour. The defects were part and parcel of English county cricket at the present day.

The chain is as strong as its weakest link. When the average of English everyday cricket is good all-round we shall find a good England team, and not before then.

Requiring 89 for his first Test match century, Fleet-wood-Smith took guard twice in the first two overs of the third day. He opened with a masterly single, then achieved an anatomical bye through the slips. A four to leg by McCormick caused the women to scream like the noises in a jungle. Fleetwood-Smith next received the ball on parts of his body irrelevant to the stroke in view. He got out in an effort to disperse the Press box, and was bowled amid cheers and merriment. The radio celebrated his innings by selections from *Chu Chin Chow*.

Australia scored 600 in 600 minutes, which was a case of exceeding the speed limit of Test matches. Farnes's analysis told of much clever and resolute bowling. England was not blessed with fortune during Australia's innings. The missed chance by Allen at the outset of McCabe's innings probably was crucial, and the irony is that Allen's fielding at forward leg throughout the tour was brilliant. He took blinding catches in this position.

At twelve-thirty England's long journey began. Showers of rain in the night had not hurt the wicket, but the day's temperature was more friendly to the bowlers than Friday's sunshine. Barnett drove McCormick's first ball beautifully to the off boundary, cut his second graciously for four through the slips, and was missed fourth ball by O'Reilly in the slips, an easy chance from a ball that reared late to the top of the bat. From the next ball, which also described an outward angle, Worthington sliced dangerously behind the wicket. It was a most eventful and emotional over.

Nash galloped violently over the earth at the other

end. Worthington hit him through the covers for three and Barnett again drove to the off for four, easy and dashing. At the end of two overs England were 25. I received the sensation of a bottle of champagne being uncorked abruptly and fizzing all over the place.

The pace was too heavy to last. Barnett flicked recklessly at an offside good-length ball at the beginning of Nash's second over, and Oldfield caught him with alacrity. This wicket was thrown away, and accepted without thanks. Nobody in a Test wishes to witness net-practice; the finest stroke-player must watch the ball, especially while it is new, until the foundation of an innings has been laid. I regret the platitude; the circumstance enforces it. The length of Nash and McCormick was what, in these days, is called legitimate. No palpable bumper occurred; this was good-mannered fast bowling which observed the unwritten ruling of the Council of Trent Bridge. But nobody liked it.

A steadier note was given to England's innings by Hardstaff and Worthington, who both put rational bats to the attack. O'Reilly came on and opened with a leg-theory maiden. Hardstaff turned Nash twice to leg with the quickest and prettiest flexion of the wrists; he promised to give a faithful account at last of his proper and fine natural ability. In forty-five minutes 53 were scored, whereupon Fleetwood-Smith began jauntily to swing his arms and lend gyrations to his wrist, apparently to a comic song of his own composition. He is a comedian and a character, and has that touch of melancholy which is in the true comedian's temperament.

Another stroke to leg by Hardstaff, this time from O'Reilly, was an adornment to the game, charming in poise and lightness of touch. I felt now that England would need to bat badly to score less than 450, a total which, on the glorious wicket, would not be worth more than 300 at Lord's.

After lunch, the crowd had a magnificent size; from the distance it looked as tidy as a clipped hedge. Hardstaff and Worthington were steady, as if realizing England's opportunity. Nash bowled at the pavilion end, but in spite of his endeavour, he could not achieve the speed that compels a batsman to hasten his stroke. Fast bowling in Australia, or rather the attempt at it, can often seem a sort of insanity, and certifiable as such.

No wicket looked in danger of falling until another cruel blow of fortune interrupted England's progress. Worthington, whose innings wore a more and more persistent aspect every minute, was out atrociously. He hit Fleetwood-Smith to leg cleanly, and disturbed his wicket as he swung round in the rhythm of a good stroke. Everyone was sorry to see such an end to Worthington's admirable cricket. Still, one should not tread on one's wicket in a Test match. Bradman doesn't.

England were 96 for two when Hammond came in to applause; no English crowd could have welcomed him with a warmth more generous. Two wickets had been given to Australia, one by Barnett's impetuosity, the other by the fates. Fleetwood-Smith pitched a reasonably accurate length, but compared to his fell work at Adelaide, his spin seemed amiable. The wicket drew his fangs. I was reminded of the snakes which the music-hall magicians dangle decoratively around their necks. The wicket was a feather bed, inert as sleep. To bowl on it was to learn patience, philosophy, resignation.

Hammond and Hardstaff risked nothing. This partnership was vital. They waited for the ball to drop in the anaesthetic bed of the earth, and played with time to spare. The crowd's attention wandered in the drowsy afternoon; the cricket became motion seen as though in a dream. When a sudden spinner from Fleetwood-Smith eluded Hardstaff's bat, the entire field jumped in surprise. The main purpose of the batsmen was to avoid mistakes. And so the match extended itself, over by over, until imagination saw it as a sort of creeping monster, feeding on itself, existing by accretion.

In the last over before tea the inevitable mistake was made, and for England it was terrible. Hammond hooked a ball from O'Reilly round to square leg. He succumbed in much the same fashion at Adelaide. It was another instance of faltering concentration. The stroke did not rise, and even as Hammond made it he must have cursed himself. Another gift to Australia, and to say this much is not to belittle the persistent steadiness of the attack. The truth is, as I have suggested, that on the wicket a deadly ball was almost beyond mortal skill. England had been playing for the last week or two like a team weary of cricket. Between lunch and tea I felt a want of policy in the batting, some indecision whether to play an abnormally dour game or a game rather at the extreme of dourness.

When the total was 130 for three, each batsman out had contributed to his own downfall, though perhaps that is a hard thing to say of the unlucky Worthington. But not one of them had been technically bowled or defeated. Immediately after tea, we actually saw Leyland cleanly and definitely bowled by a good length from O'Reilly. Leyland played over it late, and it was not a resolute stroke. Fleetwood-Smith earned high praise for his control of length. Though the wicket robbed him of his Adelaide venom, he did much to compensate himself by skilful, curving devices

through the air. He was seldom loose. And O'Reilly rolled
them over with the tireless reliability of a machine.

Bad light stopped play at the afternoon's fall, and
interrupted, or relieved, a dogged partnership between
Hardstaff and Wyatt—a forlorn hope if ever there was one.

---

### FOURTH AND FIFTH DAYS

#### AUSTRALIA First Innings

| | |
|---|---:|
| J. H. Fingleton, c. Voce, b. Farnes | 17 |
| K. E. Rigg, c. Ames, b. Farnes | 28 |
| D. G. Bradman, b. Farnes | 169 |
| S. J. McCabe, c. Farnes, b. Verity | 112 |
| C. L. Badcock, c. Worthington, b. Voce | 118 |
| R. Gregory, c. Verity, b. Farnes | 80 |
| W. A. Oldfield, c. Ames, b. Voce | 21 |
| L. J. Nash, c. Ames, b. Farnes | 17 |
| W. J. O'Reilly, b. Voce | 1 |
| E. L. McCormick, not out | 17 |
| L. O'B. Fleetwood-Smith, b. Farnes | 13 |
| Extras (b. 1, l.b. 5, n.b. 4, w. 1) | 11 |

Total . . . . . . 604

Australia first-innings bowling analysis

| | O. | M. | R. | W. |
|---|---|---|---|---|
| Allen | 17 | 0 | 99 | 0 |
| Farnes | 28·5 | 5 | 96 | 6 |
| Voce | 29 | 3 | 123 | 3 |
| Hammond | 16 | 1 | 62 | 0 |
| Verity | 41 | 5 | 127 | 1 |
| Worthington | 6 | 0 | 60 | 0 |
| Leyland | 3 | 0 | 26 | 0 |

Fall of the wickets:

| 1 | 2 | 3 | 4 | 5 | 6 | 7 | 8 | 9 | 10 |
|---|---|---|---|---|---|---|---|---|---|
| 32 | 54 | 303 | 346 | 507 | 544 | 563 | 571 | 576 | 604 |

#### ENGLAND First Innings

| | |
|---|---:|
| Barnett, c. Oldfield, b. Nash | 18 |
| Worthington, hit wicket, b. Fleetwood-Smith | 44 |
| Hardstaff, c. McCormick, b. O'Reilly | 83 |
| Hammond, c. Nash, b. O'Reilly | 14 |

ENGLAND First Innings—*continued*

Leyland, b. O'Reilly . . . . . 7
R. E. S. Wyatt, c. Bradman, b. O'Reilly . . 38
Ames, b. Nash . . . . . . 19
G. O. Allen, c. Oldfield, b. Nash . . . 0
Verity, c. Rigg, b. Nash . . . . . 0
Voce, st. Oldfield, b. O'Reilly . . . . 3
K. Farnes, not out . . . . . . 0
    Extras (l.b. 12, n.b. 1) . . . . 13

        Total . . . . . . 239

England first-innings bowling analysis

|              | O.   | M. | R. | W. |
|--------------|------|----|----|----|
| McCormick    | 13   | 1  | 54 | 0  |
| Nash         | 17·5 | 1  | 70 | 4  |
| O'Reilly     | 23   | 7  | 51 | 5  |
| Fleetwood-Smith | 18 | 3  | 51 | 1  |

Fall of the wickets:

| 1  | 2  | 3   | 4   | 5   | 6   | 7   | 8   | 9   | 10  |
|----|----|-----|-----|-----|-----|-----|-----|-----|-----|
| 33 | 96 | 130 | 140 | 202 | 236 | 236 | 236 | 239 | 239 |

ENGLAND Second Innings

Barnett, l.b.w., b. O'Reilly . . . . 41
Worthington, c. Bradman, b. McCormick . . 6
Hardstaff, b. Nash . . . . . . 1
Hammond, c. Bradman, b. O'Reilly . . . 56
Leyland, c. McCormick, b. Fleetwood-Smith . 28
R. E. S. Wyatt, run out . . . . . 9
Ames, c. McCabe, b. McCormick . . . 11
G. O. Allen, c. Nash. b. O'Reilly . . . 7
Verity, not out . . . . . . 2
Voce, c. Badcock, b. Fleetwood-Smith . . 1
K. Farnes, c. Nash, b. Fleetwood-Smith . . 0
    Extras (l.b. 3) . . . . . 3

        Total . . . . . . 165

England second-innings bowling analysis

|              | O. | M. | R. | W. |
|--------------|----|----|----|----|
| McCormick    | 9  | 0  | 33 | 2  |
| Nash         | 7  | 1  | 34 | 1  |
| O'Reilly     | 19 | 6  | 58 | 3  |
| McCabe       | 1  | 0  | 1  | 0  |
| Fleetwood-Smith | 13 | 3 | 36 | 3 |

Fall of the wickets:

| 1 | 2 | 3 | 4 | 5 | 6 | 7 | 8 | 9 | 10 |
|---|---|---|---|---|---|---|---|---|----|
| 9 | 10 | 70 | 121 | 142 | 142 | 153 | 162 | 165 | 165 |

A storm in the night threatened a bad wicket for England. Fortune played a game with Allen this rubber. She came to him with hands full of gifts, 'You shall bat first in two matches, and I'll send convenient rain for you and your bowlers. Two victories will garland your brow at Christmas.' She led him to the summit to see the rosy prize. And then she tripped him at the pinch.

The ball did not behave unreasonably to begin with on the fourth morning; but the fear that it might do so before long had an influence on the batsmen's composure, and Hardstaff set about making hay while the sun shone, or, rather, while it did not shine. He drove beautifully to the off, flicked to leg, and generally hurried himself. He was caught at mid-on aiming for another four. The ball lifted gently, enough to change a good stroke into a fatal stroke. Still, as I say, the wicket, so far, remained more or less quiescent. Hardstaff deserved his first hundred against Australia in a Test match. His innings throughout was cultured and handsome. Another irony for Allen that Hardstaff should find true form too late in the day.

Bradman rested O'Reilly and gave his attack to the fast bowlers, a sign that the ball was still coming through slowly. Wyatt played well. Though the dead outfield stole value from hits, England scored 50 in as many minutes.

At one o'clock O'Reilly came on again, and in his first over Wyatt had to be quick to counter a certain speed from the earth, from which bits and pieces were being knocked over after over. Most of us felt now that England were about to pass through another lively hour or two before the day was done. But it was not the turf that settled Ames. He was almost yorked  Wyatt was caught a yard or so from the bat. Here was the dread sign, the 'black spot'.

Silly point and silly mid-on crouched on the edge of the pitch when Verity began his innings. He scarcely saw a bowler's pitch in Australia this season except when he was batting. Allen endeavoured to smite a six. Poor Allen! The sad falling light of the lost cause had now fallen on him, making him look heroic. The crowd gave him sympathetic applause as he walked the long lonely way back to the pavilion. None the less this first innings collapse was mainly psychological. Not until one o'clock did the bowling gather energy and guile from the wicket.

Bradman, of course, invited England to bat again, and two wickets were lost at once to the fast bowlers. Worthington stupendously sent the ball straight as a tower to mid-wicket, where Bradman waited and caught it with nice judgment. A yorker scattered Hardstaff's stumps. These further disasters to England were also the consequence of the doubt which enveloped the batsmen's minds. The wicket was getting nastier minute by minute, but only now and again did the really difficult ball occur. In the circumstances a stroke could not be made confidently; it was born in dubiety.

Hammond, much more himself than he was yesterday, turned Nash to leg. All the runs England scored now were as the pagan eating and drinking before the luxury of woe and death. From the edge of the field, it was not easy to speak positively of the wicket. Most balls, as I say, came through decently enough; it was the odd one that could not be trusted. And the Australian attack contained no Verity; Fleetwood-Smith prefers a dusty pitch. There was, of course, no relation between this wicket and the spitting grill on which England were trapped at Melbourne in January. Still, it was a misfortune for England to find even an unreliable turf, so soon after yesterday's comfortable couch of runs, on which Hammond, Leyland, and Barnett missed ripe opportunities.

Barnett this time batted in his soundest and most handsome vein. An off drive from O'Reilly was a model of poise. Then he swung him for a glorious six—and was leg-before next ball to a clever and quick variation. Here was an instance of good bowling under heavy fire.

Hammond sent some noble strokes over the field. The calm ease of them suggested a firm, classical pillar, still standing erect among England's crumbling foundations. When the total reached 100, Fleetwood-Smith had not bowled. I thought this was a curious neglect, for though the conditions were probably not the kind he would himself have chosen, there was certainly a chance for spin. Fleetwood-Smith was put on after tea, and an over of meandering long-hops justified Bradman's view of his powers for the occasion, in practice at any rate if not in theory. Hammond pulled him to leg and reached a magnificent 50, another taste of gall for Allen. This innings should have been played in the first innings for England, when Hardstaff was Hammond's companion.

O'Reilly bowled resourcefully, and a ball here and there spat or hastened from the ground. On the whole, though, the pitch appeared now to be trying to reform itself, rather like the converted burglar who only occasionally helps himself to a spoon or two at a tea-party. At half-past four the old reprobate lost grace again, and Hammond fell to a ball which popped villainously. Hammond made a good royal end.

A dazzling piece of stumping by Oldfield from a beautiful spinner by Fleetwood-Smith nearly finished Leyland, but Leyland was as quick as Oldfield. Next ball Leyland was caught off a bump ball, and he made signs of chagrin and pretended to walk away. This is a good old wheeze and never fails to get a laugh anywhere between Brisbane and Bradford. These incidents enlivened the languishing day. Nothing mattered now, save the figure and the final reckoning for Mr. Ferguson's immaculate book-keeping. Wyatt batted as if determined to make a draw by some miraculous means. He was run out grievously, and as he returned to the pavilion, the radio urgently asked Doctor Mendelssohn to come forward. Probably he was wanted to compose a funeral march or mass for England.

# CHAPTER XV

## THE VERDICT

AFTER the fifth Test match had been lost and won, G. O. Allen addressed the crowd at Melbourne and said he was a sad and disappointed man. And the crowd sincerely grieved with him. I make that remark knowing that more cant is written and spoken of cricket than of any other game in the world. Australia wanted badly to win the rubber—of course they did. The crowds in Australia have not yet attained to the sublime detachment which marks the crowds at Sheffield and Maidstone, where the best (or better) side always wins as a matter of course. But though the Australian crowds expressed unashamed joy at their team's recovery and victories, they were sorry for Allen and they would have found consolation in his pleasure if they had watched the prize go to England. The average Australian's knowledge of the game is closer than the average Englishman's; nine times out of the ten he is a player or has been a player. He lacks the Englishman's sentimentality, for if a celebrated Australian cricketer begins to lose form nobody whitewashes that form. Even Bradman is not above criticism; after the second Test match in which Bradman scored o and 82, I heard many strong opinions to the effect that the great man was on the downward path. At Melbourne Sievers took five wickets for 21, but no regrets were heard when he was immediately afterwards dropped from the Australian team. Suppose, say, Smith of Middlesex were to take five for 21 for England and then become one of the rejected; severe letters would appear in the Press denouncing an outrage and an injustice. As a people we love the declining hero; we take to our hearts the singer who has lost his voice (sometimes probably to his advantage as a singer) and the cricketer who has lost his form. The Australians take a serious view of the game; it is for them worth playing well in the lowest as well as in the highest class. Mr. Milne could not have written about his 'Rabbits' in Australia; there is no room there for the duffer. Maybe the Australian misses much because of his devotion to an ideal of technical perfection, but he escapes the sloppiness of outlook which sometimes causes cricket in England to appear unctuous to mere footballers, jockeys, tennis players, and throwers of the dart. The men who did well for Allen were enormously admired by Australian crowds. Hammond seldom, if ever, receives in England the reception he is given by Sydney; the applause there follows him to the wicket and ends in rounds of cheers. The bowling of Voce, in the first and second Test matches, was toasted vociferously in the largest bar in the world, which is situated within the Australian Hotel in Castlereagh Street. Barnett was as popular as McCabe. But Australians were as a whole as perplexed and saddened as Allen himself over the failures of Hardstaff, Fagg, Worthington, Fishlock, and others. I was occasionally asked what was the state of English first-class cricket to-day that this player or that could have risen to a high place in our averages, so palpably out of his element had this or that player been revealed the moment a Test match began. I confess I could not satisfactorily answer the question, for the reason that the standards of cricket day by day in England are at the moment poor and unreliable. Once on a time we could be certain of the skill and pedigree of any batsman who scored an innings of 300 in a first-class engagement; such a score

before the war called for the organized technique and the
long experience of W. G. Grace, or Hayward, or MacLaren,
or Ranjitsinhji, or Trumper, or C. B. Fry. Nowadays it is
possible for R. H. Moore of Hampshire to make 300 in a
day, and nobody would claim that Moore is a master.
Last year Duckfield of Glamorganshire was equal to 280
not out against Surrey. Even J. T. Tyldesley, who loved
batting at Kennington Oval, never got as high as 280
against Surrey. There is not a single great fast bowler in
England at the present time; most of them bowl short.
Farnes is the best of the lot, because he tries to make the
batsman play forward. There is not a single great fast
bowler in Australia, if it comes to that. But there is spin
there and length. More important, first-class cricket in
Australia is always fresh; it is so seldom played. The
paradox is that in a country where the game is a national
passion not as many first-class matches are played in a
long season as in England we witness in a fortnight.
There is little evening practice and no mid-week club
games. But the technique of the Grade cricket is kept high
by the presence in it of Test match men. Suppose Hammond or Hardstaff were to play in Saturday afternoon
cricket in and around London. Each would achieve an
average of over a hundred, and leave far behind the
performances of his club-mates. McCabe plays Saturday
cricket for his club in Sydney; also Badcock, Bradman, and
the rest. But only Bradman scores in Grade cricket at an
abnormal average. McCabe and Fingleton do not leave
behind them in performance their ordinary and unknown
colleagues. The general standard of Grade cricket is high.
Every player, no matter how modest, is constantly toeing
the one general line of efficiency. If an Australian batsman
is capable of making a hundred in an inter-State match, his

quality can more or less be taken for granted; he has earned
his diploma. It is because a first-class match in Australia is
always an event that it is always a challenge, never a routine
job of work. Consequently the cricket is more tightly
organized tactically as well as technically than it is in
English County cricket, where on many a dog-day the
game appears to move by itself, or by the efforts of a single
great player. As the famous British conductor once said:
'This ensemble is not altogether this morning, gentlemen!'
For my part I love a view of cricket which leaves room for
easeful summertime amenities; I love to laugh if a man
misses a catch. But also I believe that a Test match should
strike fire out of a cricketer, inspire him beyond his
common stature. Aubrey Faulkner once said that the
difference between English and Australian cricketers, taking
them by and large, was that the Australian in a Test match
is a better player than usually he is—and the Englishman
slightly worse. Why is it that even against New Zealand
some of our most dashing batsmen seem to lose heart and
the use of their legs? Why, in Australia, did Fishlock and
Hardstaff—and even at last Hammond himself—become
terribly self-conscious at the sight of a slow leg-break?
Australian batsmen do not decline on firm principle to
hit the loose ball in Test matches. In the fifth Test match
of these series, the match for the rubber at Melbourne,
young Badcock scored a brilliant hundred. He was not
only taking part in a crucial engagement. He had failed at
Brisbane and Sydney and had been dropped. He was now
faced with two terribly responsible jobs—to play for
Australia, and for his position in the next Australian team
to go to England. Another failure would deprive him of
the greatest honour that can come to any Australian (not
excluding that of being Prime Minister). But Badcock did

not dither or cut out his strokes. He attacked the bowling and showed his character. Few Australian cricketers have failed in Test matches suggesting that they do not like them; it is usually possible to account for an Australian's poor form in a Test match in strict technical terms. The discrepancies shown by one or two of Allen's men, between their form in County and Test matches, was a problem not for the student of cricket, but for the psychologist. No wonder poor Gubby was rendered a sad man. He saw his team win the first two Tests; he saw his principal batsman put on the heights with four hundreds in consecutive innings, followed by 231 not out in the second Test match. Then within a few weeks the advantage was taken from him; he saw his team suddenly become chapfallen, with his principal batsman bowed down, hesitant, almost strokeless. I confess that this falling-away sickened me, and nerved me out of the godlike detachment which is supposed to govern observation from the Press box. For the failure, as Australians realistically perceived and as they frankly stated—though in different words, was, at the pinch, a failure as much of character as of technique.

## CHAPTER XVI

# BRADMAN AND HAMMOND

THE two great batsmen of the day are, of course, Bradman and Hammond. Two citizens held argument in the streets at Melbourne on New Year's Day; it was settled by force because, no doubt, it became more metaphysical than language could stand. If I were to be asked to make a decision on the point—which of the two batsmen is the greater—I should vote for Bradman on a good wicket. I do not say that Bradman cannot cope with a bad wicket, but up to now he has failed to do so in my presence. There is not the slightest doubt that Bradman, given opportunities to practise on bad wickets, would master the technique needed; in fact his flexible style, his quickness of foot, are born, so to say, for the turning ball. He is a much more dynamic player than Hammond, whose methods seem often to me to be static, with genius transforming to greatness a conventional classicism. The innings of Hammond on the impossible pitch at Melbourne could not have been excelled by any other cricketer, for balance, poise, science, and constitutionalism in conditions which were revolutionary and disruptive. But though Hammond stayed in an hour and a half that day, he scored only 35; and all the time the wicket was getting more and more impossible.

The difference between Bradman and Hammond can be stated in a few words: Hammond can be kept quiet, Bradman never. Hammond in the Test match at Sydney batted nearly eight hours; and even on the third morning, when he was still not out, he had not made England safe. Bradman in the same time would have put all bowling to rout. At Adelaide, when Australia began their second innings, everybody knew that the match and the rubber depended on Bradman. England enjoyed a slight lead; a failure by Bradman would put the issue beyond question. Bradman played carefully—for him. Allen set a wide protective field, and Bradman declined to do anything silly or rhetorical. I was writing for evening papers in Australia, and I had to send messages away every half hour. As I saw Bradman putting his bat to the ball, with a short 'lift up', body near the line, I wrote something to this effect: 'It will be a pity if Test matches are going to ruin even the stroke-play of Bradman.' At the end of an hour Bradman was 50— and not once a single flash or thump or flourish. Without his major hits, without risk or hurry, he can score faster, over a long period, than any other batsman in the game at the present time. I think he is a finer player to-day than ever he has been: he was, I thought in Australia, just beginning (so to speak) to see the ball. Once he had got over the difficulties which beset him at the beginning of the tour, his confidence in himself was terrifying in its quiet modesty. If I had to choose a batsman to play for my life, on a good wicket, I should of course name Bradman— and after doing so, I should take out an annuity.

At Adelaide, in November, on a night I shall never forget, he told me of his plans to win the rubber. He expected that O'Reilly would tie up Hammond by a leg-stump attack of good length. For the whole evening he discussed cricket—we were alone in his house. At eleven o'clock he told me he would have to turn me out, as he had a call to make at the hospital. But as the hospital was on the way to my hotel, he drove me into Adelaide, on a night of great beauty. He ran up the steps of the hospital and I waited in the car. After a short while he came back, took the wheel and said: 'I'm afraid the poor little chap isn't going to get through.' The next morning the death of Bradman's baby was announced.

I hope I am reticent enough about this night's happenings; I hope nobody will misunderstand me. I want to give an idea of Bradman's character. I am tired of hearing him referred to as a run-making machine on the field, and a hard Australian off it. (In any case, are there no 'hard' Englishmen between Newcastle, Huddersfield, and the City?) To return to our discussion of his cricket: when does a batsman who commands all the strokes and plays them rapidly and scores 300 in a day in a Test match, when does he cease to be an artist and degenerate into a 'machine'? I suppose this unintelligent objection to Bradman is much the same as the objection to Bach; it is excusable in fallible humanity to regard the illusion of mastery as bloodless and remote and automatic. But Bradman, like Bach—if he will allow the comparison—is full of blood; no other batsman to-day is as audacious as Bradman. His hook is the most dramatic hit seen since Jessop; it is a boxer's blow. And for all the rare organization of his technique, nature is in it always. Bradman has not allowed enormous skill to ruin the salt touch of his original self. The *gamin* comes out in a sudden cross-bat solecism.

When I arrived in Adelaide in November, Bradman assured me that he did not intend to score 'any more two hundreds in Test matches'. He thought there were other batsmen in the Australian team ('If ever you see Ray Robinson and myself batting at the same time, you'll forget me, and remember only *his* shots, when the day's finished'); he wished to enjoy himself. As events turned out

Bradman was compelled again to shoulder responsibility. Before the fifth Test match began in February, I saw Bradman one evening outside Usher's Hotel in Sydney; I chaffed him about the promise he had made in November. 'Well', he said, 'whose fault is it? You'll have to admit that I got out at Brisbane in the first innings having a crack; and that at Sydney in the second innings, and at Adelaide in the first, I tried to hit the ball over the on boundary. But I'm not a fool. When the English field was set to save fours —well, I wasn't going to risk a hook for nothing. I believe I've taken my reasonable chances in Tests and nobody can say that I've ever turned down a reasonable challenge to score quickly. I like to hit the ball about. But a run-saving field, everybody deep, was no good, and I reckon a good player can score fifty an hour by twos and threes if the field is scattered.'

There is a thoughtfulness in all that Bradman does, save in moments when he seems to rebel against his own mastery, as he did in England at the beginning of the season of 1934. His cricket for weeks that year was hectic; he seemed to try to hit every ball past mid-on, off the back foot, a punch not a stroke. But at the crisis he was ready, cool and grim. Australia lost three wickets for 39 at Leeds, and next morning Bradman drove Bowes's first two balls straight for four. 'Hello!' somebody said: 'The little ass is going mad again.' But the two drives had been made with the body so close to the ball that I knew the worst was coming. I fancy I can read Bradman well; I lived much with him through his difficulties of 1934. I can 'sense' a big score from him. And he has never yet failed Australia whenever it has been necessary that he should play an innings, and not merely of a hundred but one of two or three hundred. Concentration is the main reason of his mastery; that of course added to a superb technique. His strokes cover the whole field. At Leeds in 1930, after he had scored 304 in a day—a hundred before lunch, a hundred between lunch and tea, and a hundred between tea and close of play—a writer on cricket stated that Bradman had few strokes on the offside in front of the wicket. A diagram of his strokes that day was like the spokes of a bicycle wheel, or rather, like the old advertisements of electric belts with rays of vitality flashing out everywhere. No innings played by anybody, 'alive or dead' (I am reminded of Horowitz, but this is a joke secret to my friends), has exceeded in brilliant stroke-play, in combined audacity and skill, the hundred which Bradman made one Saturday evening at Lord's, against Middlesex, in 1934. What on earth do people mean when they say that Bradman is mechanical? Of the two batsmen, Bradman and Hammond, I should say that Hammond is the one more likely to dull the mind by monotony, by the suggestion of habitual professional efficiency, stately and not variegated, and never explosive.

It has been said that Bradman does not 'like' fast bowling. Once on a time I shared for a moment the same doubt. In 1930, at Liverpool, Bradman moved a yard—across to the offside—and allowed a terrific breakback from McDonald to bowl him. At the time I wrote a rather severe criticism of this piece of poor cricket. Again, in 1930, at the Oval, Bradman was seen once or twice to retreat from Larwood. But this time the retreat was away to the leg-stump, and Bradman usually tried a cut, or a hit to the off. During the 'body-line' campaign in Australia, some of us tried from this country to reconstruct what was happening whenever we read that Bradman was 'running away'. I risked the opinion that Bradman had declined to be enchained in the leg-trap. Like a great player, he sought to solve the problem by creative batsmanship; he moved aside on quick feet, and *cut* or slashed the fast bowling, which was head high three or four balls an over, sending his strokes to the vacant off-side field. It is silly to say: 'He didn't intend to get hit, or to settle down'.' Body-line', bowled at Larwood's pace, allowed no batsman to settle down. The truth is admitted now by the majority of cricketers in England that 'body-line' made batsmanship almost impossible, and that nobody but Bradman, of contemporary players, could have driven it to the offside, and scored against it at an average of 56. Against Larwood and the leg-trap, Bradman is still supposed by many folks to have failed; his scores against 'body-line' in the Test matches were 0, 103 not out, 8, 66, 76, 24, 48, and 71. In all Test matches, against England, South Africa, and the West Indies, Bradman's scores in Test matches take the breath away : 18, 1, 79, 112, 40, 58, 123, 37 not out, 8, 131, 254, 1, 334, 14, 232, 4, 25, 223, 152, 43, 0, 226, 112, 2, 167, 299 not out, 0, 103 not out, 8, 66, 76, 24, 48, 71, 38, 0, 0, 82, 13, 270, 26, 212, and 169.

The point is that this incredible sequence of scores has not been done by slow covetous cricket, but in every instance by strokes powerful, supple, swift. He cannot be kept quiet. If, as often happens, people say: 'Oh, but he hasn't the charm of McCabe, or the mercury of Macartney, or the dignity of Hammond', the objection is a little unintelligent, as though a lion were criticized for lacking the delicacy of the gazelle, the worrying tenacity of the terrier, and the disdainful elegance of a swan or a camel. Or we might as well sigh, at Bayreuth, not for the sweep and dynamic energy of Wagner, but for the poignant delicacy of Mozart as heard in the Residenztheater of Munich. We must pick and choose—and all sorts are needed to make the world's fairground. 'He's the best I ever saw,' said Wilfred

Rhodes to me a year or two ago; then he shrewdly modified the opinion, as he of course would—'He's the best back-foot player I ever saw.' Bradman is seldom, if ever, detected in the act of playing forward 'full-stretch'. That is another of his secrets; he sees the ball so quickly, so soon and so late, that he is only at rare intervals—once or twice in a season—in the wrong position when the ball pitches. It is almost impossible to bowl a difficult length to him; in fact, whatever you bowl is usually wrong. He is a ruthless critic of himself and of others. At Melbourne, after the fifth Test match, we spoke together of Worthington's wretched luck. Worthington had gone through the tour without a decent score in a Test match, but at last he found form, played as though about to get a century and trod on his wicket at 44, while performing a splendid hook. 'Yes', said Bradman, 'he was playing well, and it *was* a shame.' Then, after a pause—'Still, you know, a batsman *shouldn't* tread on his wicket.' A terrible little man, but likeable, and with a wistful something about him, probably that melancholy which Aristotle says is the mark of all the great ones of the earth.

Hammond was, in his first years of county cricket, a stroke-player of audacity. He came to Old Trafford one Whitsuntide and hooked Macdonald many times in an innings of nearly two hundred. In those days Lancashire had one or two old soldiers of bowlers who knew how to check strokes. But nobody could stop the course of Hammond that day. He was, as a young man, so rapid and brilliant a player that a member of the Selection Committee of the period assured me that Hammond was too reckless for a Test match cricketer. In the passing of time, Hammond grew older and conformed to the Test match policy which was enforced under D. R. Jardine, a grim policy indeed, which, in Australia especially, distrusted all strokes not controlled cannily. I believe that Hammond is the only contemporary English batsman who could go, without fear of becoming anonymous by contrast, into the company of MacLaren, Trumper, Tyldesley, Hutchings, and others. But also I believe that under MacLaren's captaincy, Hammond would have remained to the end a match-winning Test match batsman, an annihilator of all bowling, not only a beautiful stylist, weighted with responsibility, and glad of an escape into the gentler atmosphere of Gloucestershire cricket. For it is to the Hammond of county matches that we have had usually to look for the free and happy Hammond. In Test matches he has often seemed to carry the whole weight of his side's responsibilities, and though the burden has not submerged his genius it has subdued his spirit. The Australians set themselves to 'keep him quiet'. On good wickets they were satisfied not to try particularly to get him out so long as they checked his hits. A sort of a compliment, after all. But though my admiration of Hammond as a batsman is second to none—not to admire him would be myopic and idiotic—I sometimes feel sadly that circumstances have hindered his proper way of development. He belongs, in his methods, to the Golden Age, the pre-war period when we did not consider it criminal for a player to get caught at long-on in a Test match for less than two hundred.

# CHAPTER XVII

# DIGRESSION ON LARWOOD

WHEREVER I travelled in Australia, I heard praise of Larwood; also I heard expressions of regret that he was not with us now. He was not blamed for his contribution to the 'body-line' controversy, which was caused by a form of attack now condemned by nearly all English players actively taking part in first-class cricket. 'Larwood did a job of work under instructions'—that was the Australian comment in all places between Perth and Woolloongabba. Larwood's attack was first admired in Australia when he bowled at Brisbane and shot wickets down one after another. Chapman won the match by nearly 700 runs—and Larwood was hailed as the finest fast bowler from England in living memory. Hence the tribute I have now written and not, I hope, irrelevantly included in this book.

From time to time the glossy moral unction of the game is temporarily rubbed off by some savage who has more energy than is good for him. He rushes into the drawing-room and, before he can be stopped, he is on the royal hearthrug; and the ruling caste of the Dedlocks turns faint with horror. In the 'eighties or early 'nineties the professionals went on strike for more money. 'Good heavens', spluttered the Dedlocks, 'more money? What do they want it for?' In our own time the traces have been kicked over by Parkin; by that beautiful cricketer Jack Newman, who actually kicked the wicket over in public view under the eyes of Lord Tennyson; and by the great Cid of cricket,

A. W. Carr. These men would not, could not, toe the conventional line; how they embarrassed the upholders of taste! They made it hard for the Dedlocks to open their annual cricket-club bazaars with the old Talk about 'Playing cricket'—'It's not cricket'—as though cricketers came before footballers and jockeys in the eyes of the Lord.

Then Larwood threw his bomb. Of course we all applauded the act for a while, so long as the bomb fell in the midst of the enemy. 'Body-line' was the nation's answer to Bradman and his double centuries. But the worst of these stormy-petrels is that they will go on following us and screaming and flapping disturbed wings long after the unfriendly and alien seas have been left far behind and we are back in safe home waters. Larwood actually thought that what was good enough for Bradman and Australia would be considered good enough for the peaceful cricket fields of England. And so photographs were taken of the bruised anatomies of men who had fought the good fight along with Larwood in the realms of the barbarian, photographs of ribs tickled by this same Larwood, and of good honest Lancashire thighs and buttocks stamped with the name of the maker of the ball—aimed by Larwood who, demented spirit, could not make the proper English compromise at the right time. Of course, he was stopped; there is a limit. And Nature took a hand in the affair; she destroyed some secret pivotal place in Larwood's toe; she, who does not really love her own earthquakes and tidal-waves, 'larned' Larwood not to be himself in excess.

By the power of his genius Larwood gave us all a good shaking. The firing of the first cannon-ball in the history of warfare did not cause as much consternation as Larwood's first fast ball bowled past the batsman's left ear to a crouching leg-trap. Bradman sat enthroned, a Moloch easefully digesting his year's diet of poor enslaved trundlers. Larwood arrived in the burgeoning land tiny as Gulliver in Brobdingnag. In a moment the god was thrown down, by a pebble from a catapult. Think of it, the blistering Australian heat, the polished turf, the crowd ravenous for another record by Bradman. Larwood begins with the usual chaste field—four slips, cover, extra-cover, and only one man on the leg side, near the boundary and fine, to save the four. Larwood bowls a few conventional overs, formally doing homage to the new ball. Crack! bang! sounds the bat. Australia 20 for none in no time. Jardine makes the sign—the comprehensive wave of the arm that moves the four slips, and nearly everybody else, to the encircling net of the leg-side body-snatchers. 'Closer up', says Jardine to the Nawab of Pataudi, who takes a few strides nearer to the left pocket of Bradman. 'A bit closer, Pat', orders Jardine, and Pataudi sits under Bradman's chin, and notices how carefully he has shaved to-day. The thunderbolts flash through the air; the scene is suddenly changed; a few minutes ago the Australian ship prospered in calm waters; now she is sinking with all hands; holes through her sides, mainmast swept away. The perfect Sydney wicket—to try, for a change, another metaphor—was not long ago a batsman's cushion stuffed with runs; it is now a rack of nightmare. Bradman, like a man of genius, tries to retaliate, and he achieves brilliance. But the old lease at the wicket has lapsed; he is under notice to quit; each of his boundaries is a farewell supper. By strength of his right arm, and a new dodge, Larwood solves the problem of years—how to put an end to the tyranny of the perfect pitch, and the great batsman's endless reign on it. Was it not cric'et? Is there

not a higher order of ethics than the common one? But
the great ones of the earth have always been brought down
in their empyrean flights, their reckless wingings into the
sun, which blind them and make them mad—madness
being what occurs to a man who upsets the pleasant equili-
brium of things. A race of Larwoods would have wrecked
cricket, no doubt. But, by the measure of genius which is
employed by the amoral gods, Larwood's deeds in Australia
were wonderful. As I say, it was all right so long as he let
his sling go flying into the ranks of the foe. Old men in the
West End clubs staggered to their feet, seized the tongs and
the fire-irons, and demonstrated where Bradman was
wrong in technique and temperament. To-day the old men
are still warlike, with their walking-sticks and pokers,
but, as I say, no contemporary county cricketer has a word
to say on behalf of the method of attack which won the
rubber in Australia a year or two ago.

Fast bowling is dying out. There are one or two
believers yet, maybe, in the old faith, who call for four
slips and ask the wicket-keeper to stand back. But it is all
nothing but a rite performed in a temple from which the
spirit has long since fled. Batsmen play to the pretence;
they go to the wicket heavily padded, huge leg-guards,
and their bodies encased in circular wadding, until they
look like advertisements for Michelin tyres. And Gover
runs on the flat of his feet, and bowls not much faster off
the pitch than the Larwood of to-day: Larwood who now
is compelled to use the canter of compromise instead of his
old lovely gallop over the earth, head down, like a young
colt chafing his bit. In a few years from now, the modern
sceptics will deny there ever was fast bowling. We can hear
them: 'Fast bowling?—a Victorian and Edwardian crudity,
a form of the current and brutal Jingoism. We are subtler

and more sensitive, with our inswingers and googlies. Besides, were your Richardsons and Brearleys really fast? What were your standards of speed, what had you to go by? To-day we have seen the aeroplane and the breakneck velocity of the dirt-track. What did the Victorians know of pace? They used to send a man with a red flag in front of a traction engine. People used to get run over in the streets by hansom-cabs; how did they manage it? No wonder they thought Arthur Mold was quick!'

Larwood was the last of the classical fast bowlers; he showed his left side to the batsman, as Tom Richardson did. His body swung over the right hip, and his follow-through was thrilling. Even yet you can see these beauties of rhythm in his action, reduced though they are by physical hurt sustained in Australia. If ever a cricketer wore himself out in the service of his country, Larwood is his name. He stood to his guns in the face of a roaring outraged continent. And what guns they were, right or wrong. Australia has been the graveyard of fast bowlers. Take these figures, all of them epitaphs to doomed endeavour on the hard earth of Sydney, Brisbane, Adelaide, Melbourne: Richardson, average a wicket 30; Lockwood, 68; Hirst, 42; Cotter, 30; Howell of Warwickshire, 66; Gregory, 31; Macdonald, 65; Fielder, 27; Ernest Jones, 27; Frank Foster, 21. In 1928–9, Larwood's bowling analysis, for Test matches in Australia, was 18 wickets for 728 runs, average 40·44. On English wickets, in 1930, Larwood against Bradman and the Australians took four wickets for 292, in 101 overs, average 73·00. The cruel pitches frustrated him, and so the leg-trap was invented. But, as Burke pointed out, the march of the human intellect is slow.

# THE LAST CHAPTER

THE book after all has dealt mainly with cricket. I can only make a synopsis of all the things I might have written upon—the delectable things that I shall remember, long after the Test matches have gone from mind. Yet perhaps they were pleasures too naïve for writing about. I was the innocent abroad; it was my first sea voyage of any length. All my life I had been an islander in England, where a journey to the Continent is still regarded as travel. I have often astonished friends by suggesting a week-end in Vienna: 'Good God!' they have said: 'It is hundreds of miles away.' It is not as far as Adelaide is from Sydney.

When an experience has been lived through, reflection has sieved the irritants away. I do not think now of the mosquitoes, the humid weather, the occasional crudities of Australia, the heartiness of a nation not grown up, the perpetual welter of sport, the scarcity of theatres, music, and good talk. I had the luck to find in time Australia's secret. It is a mistake to go to the earth's other end to look for the kind of civilization which obtains in Europe. This is the land of the sun, the land in which to release oneself from a sickly introspection, from the squirrel's cage of sophisticated living. Australia is a happy country; it has its inferiority complex, maybe, in the presence of the English. This complex takes the form of a general drawing of one's attention to points of Australian life which make themselves known without the aid of the ubiquitous 'Best in the world!' And so many beautiful and fine things in Australia are never mentioned at all.

Heavens, how I shall miss Sydney this winter, when the cold dark days surround us in England! How I shall say, as I shiver on a bitter November morning: 'This time last year I was walking along North Terrace in Adelaide, seeking the shade of the trees, as I went to the University before the match, to hear a young girl student play César Franck.' Or—'This time last year I was laughing and joking in the bar of the Queensland Club amongst the most generous chaps I ever saw'—it could be the Adelaide Club, or Weld Club at Perth, just the same—'while outside the twilight came with cool air after a day of beaten gold.' Or—'This time last year I was riding down from Vaucluse to Sydney, and on my right was the harbour, now hidden for a moment, then appearing in some unexpected place, as it curved and glistened in the moonlight. And there the Bridge stood, as though on guard over everything, the Bridge that you are always seeing in Sydney, miles round, from all nooks and corners, the *leitmotiv* of Sydney, the theme-song of Sydney, "Our Harbour, our Bridge—and our DON!"'

I'll close my book with a few quick blissful moments of vision—far away now, far away. A soft gliding car, up beyond King's Park, Perth, on our first night in Australia, a corner of the world; we are voyagers to unknown delights, and our new-found friends take us in charge entirely, and we are in their hands and we seem to belong to all that they do or show us. . . . Collins Street on a Saturday night, stately but vacant; illuminated dignity. Melbourne is Australia with its top hat on . . . The stars in the sky anywhere over Sydney; stars are never seen in England. In Sydney, and anywhere else in Australia, they are piercing; you see the points of each star as in a child's picture. And the moon, a stage moon, painted on the purple canvas; but no, that's a vile and heavy metaphor. The new moon over Sydney is delicate as a silver horn . . . The great emptiness of Australia's interior; the signs everywhere of the sweat and labour and sacrifice of the pioneers. The city life on the edge of the continent is only the decoration on the saucer . . . The smart girls of Castlereagh Street, their cocky little white hats and coatees . . . The flower shops and the apparently mother-of-pearl taxi cabs . . . King's Cross and its Soho flavours . . . The hills beyond Adelaide and the handsome house in which we stayed and played miniature golf on the lawn . . . The palm trees in the busy streets at Sydney . . . The sense that we are at the earth's end, removed from all we have always thought was most vital and important in our lives. The kaleidoscope goes on in my mind, in my memory. Cricket in Australia. The Rubber. Perpetual sunshine. Salamanders. England two up and three to play; the happy Christmas in sunshine; then the defeat at Melbourne; the growing disillusionment; poor Gubby Allen; Bradman, Bradman, Bradman; Australia jubilant; 'Come and have a spot'; friendliness and more friendliness. And all the time, Australia herself subtly at work, changing dubious first impressions to agreeable second thoughts; then to interest, enjoyment, and, at last—in my case anyhow—to affection. I shall go there again, and on this occasion I shall enter under 'our Bridge', and arrange to be there in time for oysters and chicken at Usher's, when the two ladies who comprise the orchestra play their music, and outside the window the neon signs begin to glow.

# APPENDIX

# AVERAGES
# FOR THE FIVE TESTS

## AUSTRALIA

### BATTING

| | Inns | Times not out | Runs | Highest innings | Avge. |
|---|---|---|---|---|---|
| D. G. Bradman . | 9 | 0 | 810 | 270 | 90·00 |
| S. J. McCabe . . | 9 | 0 | 491 | 112 | 54·55 |
| R. Gregory . . | 3 | 0 | 153 | 80 | 51·00 |
| J. H. Fingleton . | 9 | 0 | 398 | 136 | 44·22 |
| A. G. Chipperfield . | 6 | 2 | 155 | 57* | 38·75 |
| C. L. Badcock . . | 4 | 0 | 128 | 118 | 32·00 |
| W. A. Brown . . | 4 | 0 | 95 | 42 | 23·75 |
| K. E. Rigg . . | 5 | 0 | 118 | 47 | 23·60 |
| L. J. Nash . . | 1 | 0 | 17 | 17 | 17·00 |
| M. Sievers . . | 6 | 1 | 67 | 25* | 13·40 |
| L. S. Darling . . | 2 | 0 | 20 | 20 | 10·00 |
| W. A. Oldfield . | 9 | 1 | 79 | 27* | 9·87 |
| L. P. O'Brien . . | 2 | 0 | 17 | 17 | 8·50 |
| E. L. McCormick . | 6 | 2 | 33 | 17* | 8·25 |
| W. J. O'Reilly . | 9 | 1 | 56 | 37* | 7·00 |
| L. O'B. F.-Smith . | 4 | 1 | 18 | 13 | 6·00 |
| F. Ward . . . | 6 | 1 | 27 | 18 | 5·40 |
| R. Robinson . . | 2 | 0 | 5 | 3 | 2·50 |

### BOWLING

| | Overs | Mdns | Runs | Wkts | Avge |
|---|---|---|---|---|---|
| Sievers . . . | 75·2 | 25 | 161 | 9 | 17·88 |
| Nash . . . | 24·5 | 2 | 104 | 5 | 20·80 |
| O'Reilly . . | 247·6 | 89 | 555 | 25 | 22·20 |
| Fleetwood-Smith . | 131·4 | 20 | 463 | 19 | 24·36 |
| McCormick . . | 84 | 6 | 316 | 11 | 28·72 |
| McCabe . . | 42 | 5 | 128 | 4 | 32·00 |
| Ward . . . | 136 | 28 | 432 | 11 | 29·27 |
| Gregory . . . | 3 | 0 | 14 | 0 | — |
| Chipperfield . . | 43 | 8 | 136 | 0 | — |

### CENTURIES

AUSTRALIA.—Fingleton 100 (first Test), 136 (third Test); Bradman 270 (third Test), 212 (fourth Test), 169 (fifth Test); McCabe 112 (fifth Test); Badcock 118 (fifth Test).

## ENGLAND

### BATTING

|  | Inns | Times not out | Runs | Highest innings | Avge |
|---|---|---|---|---|---|
| Hammond . . . | 9 | 1 | 468 | 231* | 58·50 |
| Leyland . . . | 9 | 1 | 441 | 126 | 55·12 |
| Barnett . . . | 9 | 0 | 395 | 129 | 43·88 |
| Hardstaff . . | 9 | 0 | 256 | 83 | 28·44 |
| R. E. S. Wyatt. . | 4 | 0 | 100 | 50 | 25·00 |
| R. W. V. Robins . | 6 | 0 | 113 | 61 | 18·83 |
| G. O. Allen . . | 9 | 1 | 150 | 68 | 18·75 |
| Ames . . . | 9 | 0 | 166 | 52 | 18·44 |
| Fagg . . . | 3 | 0 | 42 | 27 | 14·00 |
| Worthington . . | 6 | 0 | 74 | 44 | 12·33 |
| Verity . . . | 9 | 2 | 75 | 19 | 10·71 |
| K. Farnes . . | 4 | 3 | 7 | 7* | 7·00 |
| Voce . . . | 8 | 3 | 19 | 8 | 3·80 |
| Sims . . . | 2 | 0 | 3 | 3 | 1·50 |

### BOWLING

|  | Overs | Mdns | Runs | Wkts | Avge |
|---|---|---|---|---|---|
| Voce . . . | 162·1 | 20 | 560 | 26 | 21·53 |
| Farnes . . . | 73·3 | 8 | 256 | 11 | 23·27 |
| Hammond . . | 88·4 | 8 | 301 | 12 | 25·08 |
| Allen . . . | 128·7 | 12 | 526 | 17 | 30·34 |
| Verity . . . | 195·7 | 57 | 455 | 10 | 45·50 |
| Robins . . . | 56 | 3 | 220 | 4 | 55·00 |
| Sims . . . | 51 | 2 | 244 | 3 | 81·33 |
| Worthington . . | 10 | 0 | 78 | 0 | — |
| Barnett . . . | 5 | 1 | 15 | 0 | — |
| Leyland . . . | 5 | 0 | 32 | 0 | — |

### CENTURIES

ENGLAND.—Leyland 126 (first Test), 111* (third Test); Hammond 231* (second Test); Barnett 129 (fourth Test).